ACCEPT NO SUBSTITUTES!

The History of American Advertising

Christina Mierau

Even MARK TWAIN *would have been stumped!*

And if the tomatoes would have taxed his powers of adequate description, what of the soup itself! For Campbell's Tomato Soup, with all its individual tang and flavor, is hard indeed to put into words.

Just let it speak for itself—to your appetite and your delight in exhilarating goodness. If ever a soup appealed to your taste as being in a class by itself, this is it. "I don't know why it is so delicious or how to describe it," you will say, "but I *do* know that it is the soup for me!"

Tomato Soup when you add water. Cream of Tomato when you add milk. An irresistible delight either way!

Double rich! Double strength!

Campbell's Soups bring you condensed, concentrated goodness. So when you add an equal quantity of water in your kitchen, you obtain twice the quantity of soup at no extra cost.

21 kinds to choose from . . .

Asparagus	Clam Chowder	Noodle with chicken
Bean	Consommé	Ox Tail
Beef	Julienne	Pea
Bouillon	Mock Turtle	Pepper Pot
Celery	Mulligatawny	Printanier
Chicken	Mushroom (Cream of)	Tomato
Chicken-Gumbo	Mutton	Vegetable
		Vegetable-Beef

LOOK FOR THE RED-AND-WHITE LABEL

CAMPBELL'S TOMATO SOUP

LERNER PUBLICATIONS COMPANY • MINNEAPOLIS

For Dad, with love

Special thanks to editors Sara Saetre and Margaret Goldstein and to the staff of John W. Hartman Center at Duke University, especially Russell Koonts for graciously sharing his expertise in sales, marketing, and advertising history.

Lerner Publications Company
A Division of Lerner Publishing Group
241 First Avenue North
Minneapolis, MN 55401 U.S.A.

Website address: www.lernerbooks.com

Library of Congress Cataloging-in-Publication Data

Mierau, Christina B.
    Accept no substitutes! the history of American advertising /Christina Mierau.
        p.   cm. — (People's history)
    Includes bibliographical references and index.
    Summary: Provides a social history of advertising in America, from its origins in the 1600s to the present, showing how it has influenced and been influenced by American culture.
    ISBN 0-8225-1742-6 (lib. bdg.: alk. paper)
    1. Advertising—United States—History—Juvenile literature.
[1. Advertising—History.] I. Title: History of American advertising. II. Title. III. Series.
HF5813.U6M53   2000
659.1'0973—dc21   99-027580

Manufactured in the United States of America
1 2 3 4 5 6 – JR – 05 04 03 02 01 00

Contents

SATISFACTION GUARANTEED

Promise—large promise—is the soul of an advertisement.
   —Samuel Johnson, 1758

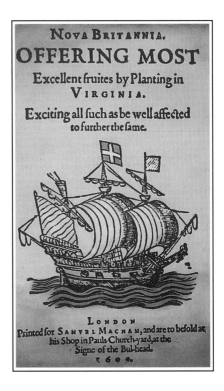

ate in August 1784, the sight of Philadelphia's bustling waterfront drew shouts of joy from the ragged men and women aboard the ship *Faithful Steward.* Their Atlantic crossing—a journey plagued by "smells, fumes, horrors, vomiting, . . . seasickness, . . . fever, dysentery, . . . and similar afflictions"—had, at last, reached its end. With renewed hope, the sea-weary Europeans looked forward to what the advertisements at home had promised. America offered land for the asking, plentiful jobs, generous wages, and seemingly unlimited opportunity. The newcomers felt certain that the difficult journey they had undertaken was well worth a share in the abundant prosperity of this sprawling new continent.

Historians have called the effort to people the American colonies the world's first large-scale advertising campaign. Powerful English trading companies, hoping to gain control of North America's vast natural resources, built settlements along its shores. The success of these colonies, however, depended on workers who could clear America's dense woodlands and cultivate its rich, fertile soil. "Lands, though excellent, without hands proportionable," wrote Englishman Josiah Child in 1664, "enhance no kingdom."

Throughout western Europe, smooth-talking promoters scoured overcrowded slums in search of men and women willing to emigrate to America. Armed with attractive handbills, posters, and pamphlets, these hired agents used half-truths, exaggeration, and often outright trickery to persuade Europe's downtrodden to seek their fortunes in North America. In public places, the agents posted large, single-sheet advertisements called broadsides that listed vessels bound for the American colonies. Even the names of the ships advertised optimism and goodwill, for one might sail to the New World on the *Friendship, Harmony, Fame,* or *Success.*

Pamphlets containing first-person accounts of life in America were among the most persuasive advertisements. England's William Penn, founder of the Pennsylvania colony, appointed his associate, Gabriel Thomas, to publicize the benefits of colonial life. In 1693 Thomas's account appeared in a widely read booklet. Of America, he wrote:

> Poor people (both Men and Women) of all kinds, can here get three times the wages for their Labour they can in England or Wales. . . . Labouring Men, Women, and Children of England, wandering up and down looking for employment, here not need idle for a moment. . . . Here there are no beggars. . . . Jealousies among Men here are rare. . . . What I have delivered . . . is indisputably true, I was an eyewitness to it all.

Carefully crafted advertisements such as this proved irresistible to those with little chance for success in their homelands. Between 1630 and 1800, some five and a half million people emigrated to the American colonies. Many found that life in America easily measured up to the recruiters' promises.

Others, however, found colonial life far different from what had been advertised. Many colonists were indentured servants, people who agreed to work in America in exchange for the cost of their passage from Europe. Some servants—those who were poorly fed, inadequately housed, or mercilessly punished by ill-tempered masters—grew disillusioned and broke their agreements by running away. Notices offering rewards for their return filled colonial newspapers. On September 28, 1784, landowner Samuel Linton advertised in the *Pennsylvania Gazette* for help in recovering his runaway servant:

> The twenty-fifth of this September,
> I would have you well remember,
> My 'prentice boy he ran away,
> Was sixteen years of age last May;
> His name James Clifft, his visage light,
> And likes to ramble in the night,
> Above five feet six inches high,
> And very apt to swear and lie,
> The smaller pox has left its trace,
> And may be seen upon his face.

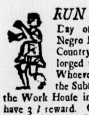

An ad in a 1774 edition of the **Charleston Gazette** promised a reward for the return of a runaway slave.

Next, I'll describe the clothes he wore,
And others that away he bore.
The coat was brown, his jacket blue,
The hat he wore was almost new.

READ ALL ABOUT IT

Settlers, having survived the challenge of the North American wilderness, watched their colonies grow in size, number, and prosperity. Travel and trade increased along the Atlantic coastline, with its deep harbors and navigable inland rivers. New Hampshire's foresters exchanged sturdy white pine for the fruits of New York's farms. Southern planters discovered that tobacco was as much in demand throughout the colonies as it was in Europe. Bridging the gap between previously isolated settlements, this brisk trade sharpened colonists' appetites for a way to tell everyone about the goods and services they had to offer.

As Boston's postmaster in 1704, John Campbell was often the first to hear current news from neighbors and arriving visitors. One of Campbell's duties was to record all this information in a handwritten report for the local English authorities. Thinking that the public might find his news digest interesting, Campbell asked his superiors for permission to publish and distribute it. The members of the Massachusetts General Court granted his request, provided that they would have full control over what he wrote. The officials feared that uncensored news might jeopardize their authority.

On April 17, 1704, the *Boston News Letter* became America's first regularly published newspaper. In the first issue, editor Campbell invited readers to advertise in the paper for a small fee:

This News Letter is to be continued Weekly, and all Persons who have any Houses, Lands, Tenements, Farmes, Vessels, Goods, Wares, or Merchandize, & cc. To be sold or Lett, or Servants Run away; or Goods Stollen or Lost, may have the same inserted at a Reasonable Rate.

A few weeks later, three paid advertisements ran in the *News Letter*. Two people sought the return of stolen property, and a third had a house to sell. America's first real estate ad offered, "At Oyster Bay, on Long Island . . . New York . . . a very good Fulling-Mill . . . also a Plantation, having on it a new Brick house."

For many colonists, the advertisements were the most entertaining part of the newspaper, certainly more interesting than outdated news from England. Advertising offered readers drama in the form of local happenings. Each ad told the tale of a runaway, of property lost or stolen, of ships arriving with goods for sale or departing for foreign ports. The advertisements of the colonial period illustrate an early American fascination for buying, selling, trading, and doing business.

However, the *Boston News Letter* lacked one very important characteristic—journalistic freedom. If the local authorities disliked something Campbell wrote, they could stop funding the paper and shut it down. No paper could be a free press—one that could print all ideas and opinions without fear of punishment—unless it could earn enough money to operate independently, without government support. Publishers soon recognized that advertising fees could help a newspaper support itself.

BENJAMIN FRANKLIN, PRINTER

In 1723, having learned the printing trade as a boy in Boston, Benjamin Franklin settled in Philadelphia and later became the editor of his own newspaper, the *Pennsylvania Gazette.* At the time, Philadelphia was America's leading economic center.

Ben Franklin wanted to make the *Gazette* a first-rate newspaper—one in which businesspeople would want to place their advertisements. His print was clear and readable, his writing style lively and entertaining. He used his profits to buy high-quality supplies and equipment. Before long more people were reading the *Pennsylvania Gazette* than any other newspaper. Advertisers who hoped to reach as many readers as possible placed their ads in the *Gazette*.

Benjamin Franklin bought a printing press in 1728. Then he started a newspaper, the **Pennsylvania Gazette,** *and ran advertisements in it.*

Franklin was both a shrewd businessman and a creative artist. In most newspapers of the time, ads appeared as endless rows of type, and every ad looked just like all the rest. By adding small, eye-catching pictures to the ads in his paper, Franklin made it easy for readers to see at a glance what was being advertised: a boat, a new pair of books, a reward for a runaway servant. Then he framed each advertisement with a blank border—called white space—that set the ad apart from the next.

Franklin, who was also a scientist and an inventor, advertised his own products as well. In a 1744 advertisement for his Pennsylvania Fireplace, Franklin offered the customer not just a household heater but also luxurious comfort, health, and peace of mind.

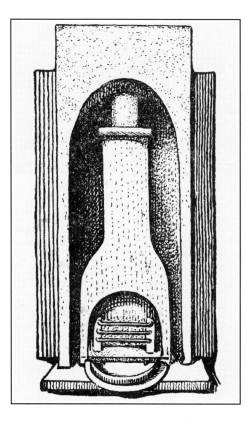

In 1744 Benjamin Franklin advertised that his fireplace not only kept cold drafts out of the house but also protected people from "the early appearance of old age."

Your whole room is equally warmed, so that people don't need to crowd so close around your fire, but may sit near the window and have the benefit of the light for reading, writing, needlework, etc. . . . You have not that cold draft of uncomfortable air nipping at your back and heels . . . by which you may catch colds . . . coughs, toothaches, fever, pleurisies, and many other diseases . . . . As very little heat is lost when this fireplace is used, much less wood will serve you, which is a considerable advantage where wood is dear. . . . And, lastly, the fire is secured at night, that not one spark can fly out of the room to do damage.

Then, using an advertising technique that is still popular, Franklin appealed to his readers' vanity. He warned them that ordinary stoves, unlike his Pennsylvania Fireplace, "would damage the eyes . . . and shrivel the skin, bringing on the early appearance of old age." Franklin's understanding of human nature sold a lot of stoves.

SIGNS OF THE TIMES

By 1750 colonial Philadelphia, with forty thousand inhabitants, ranked second only to London as the biggest city in the British kingdom. Its streets lay in tidy, parallel rows and were alive with small businesses like Benjamin Franklin's Market Street printing shop.

Philadelphia's merchants adopted a European tradition by marking their businesses with signs and logos. Some signs hung from tall, freestanding poles; others dangled from chains above doorways. Each sign announced to passersby what goods or services the shop owner offered.

Signs throughout the colonies revealed something about the people who displayed them. In New England, straitlaced Puritans hung signs that were plain and unadorned. The simple likeness of a black boot on a white plank might mark a cobbler's shop, while the village blacksmith hammered away under the sign of a horseshoe or anvil. Along New York's waterfront, tavern signs commonly featured paintings of clipper ships, mermaids, and fish that invited sailors to "Coil up your ropes and anchor here/till better weather does appear."

One early American artist named Matthew Pratt created many of the signs that decorated colonial Philadelphia. Pratt's most popular sign marked the entrance to a tavern on the corner of Fourth and Chestnut Streets. It pictured a gathering of political delegates. Passersby often stopped outside the tavern and challenged each other to see who could identify the most figures depicted on the sign. Not surprisingly, during Philadelphia's sweltering summers, the same crowds would continue their friendly competition inside the tavern— with a refreshing tankard of ale or cider. As he refilled his customers' drinks, the tavern owner realized a simple truth—it paid to advertise.

The names of inns and roadhouses in colonial America often honored England's king, George III. Names like The King's Arms and

His Majesty's Inn were popular—until the American Revolution. Then patriotic Americans hauled away signs that reminded them of England and replaced them with new ones that celebrated American independence.

In Washington Irving's folktale "Rip Van Winkle," the title character sleeps for twenty years—right through the American Revolution—and awakes to a changed village. Standing outside what had once been his favorite tavern:

> He recognized on the sign...the ruby face of King George...but...the red coat was changed for one of blue and buff, a sword was held in the hand instead of a scepter, the head was decorated with cocked hat, and underneath was painted in large characters GENERAL WASHINGTON.

In the 1770s, a sign featuring England's King George III welcomed weary sailors to King's Head tavern in New York City. Meanwhile, a placard advertised for recruits to join the Continental army.

This handbill told American colonists not to "buy any one thing" of an importer loyal to Great Britain during the American Revolution.

WILLIAM JACKSON,

an *IMPORTER*; at the

BRAZEN HEAD,

North Side of the TOWN-HOUSE,

and *Oppofite the Town-Pump, in*

Corn-hill, BOSTON.

It is defired that the SONS and
DAUGHTERS of *LIBERTY,*
would not buy any one thing of
him, for in fo doing they will bring
Difgrace upon *themfelves,* and their
Pofterity, for *ever* and *ever,* AMEN

"UNITED IN SENTIMENT"

Before the American Revolution, many colonists had questioned the wisdom of breaking ties with England. But colonial leaders like Boston's Samuel Adams used propaganda—advertising designed to change people's minds and opinions—to rally public support for the revolution. As the leader of a group of militant patriots called the Sons of Liberty, Adams hoped to plant "the seeds of rebellion" in the minds of colonial people. With handbills, posters, speeches, and newspaper ads, Adams urged people to boycott (refuse to buy) English goods. Advertisements often singled out American merchants who continued to do business with England. One ad read:

> WILLIAM JACKSON, an IMPORTER....It is desired that the SONS and DAUGHTERS of LIBERTY, would not buy any one thing of him, for in so doing they will bring Disgrace upon *themselves,* and their *Posterity,* for *ever* and *ever,* AMEN.

Samuel Adams, a leading colonial patriot, spread the word that people should boycott English goods.

Advertisements like this—read and discussed throughout the colonies—fueled a growing spirit of rebellion against the English. In 1774 Samuel Adams declared triumphantly in a letter to Benjamin Franklin, "Colony communicates freely with colony. . . . The whole continent is now becoming united in sentiment and opposed to tyranny."

Adams was not alone in using advertisements to further the cause of freedom. To encourage volunteers to join the Continental army, political leaders posted persuasive advertisements throughout the colonies:

TO ALL BRAVE, HEALTHY, ABLE BODIED, AND WELL DISPOSED YOUNG MEN. . . . Join the Troops now raising under GENERAL WASHINGTON for the defence of the LIBERTIES and INDEPENDENCE of the United States. . . . Those who . . . embrace this opportunity of spending a few happy years in viewing the different parts of this beautiful continent . . . to return home to his friends with his pockets full of money and his head covered with laurels. GOD SAVE THE UNITED STATES.

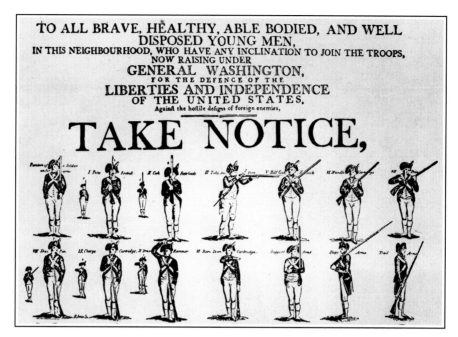

This poster appealed to manly honor, asking all "brave, healthy, able bodied, and well disposed young men" to join the U.S. infantry under George Washington.

Few soldiers returned from the war with pockets full of money and laurels on their heads, however. Like some indentured servants who had come to America seeking a better life, many of the patriots who answered Washington's call to arms discovered that advertisements sometimes promise more than they can deliver.

BUILDERS, BOOSTERS, AND BALLYHOO

Many a small thing has been made large by the right kind of advertising.
   —Mark Twain, *A Connecticut Yankee in King Arthur's Court,* 1889

George Washington folded the newspaper, set it aside on his desk, and penned a short letter to his friend Henry Knox:

> My Dear Sir:
> Having learned from an Advertisement in the New York Daily Advertiser, that there were superfine American Broad Cloths to be sold at No. 44 in Water Street, I have ventured to trouble you with... purchasing enough to make me a suit of cloathes.

Two months later—on April 30, 1789—Washington pledged the oath of office as the first president of the United States. He wore a suit of "brown Connecticut cloth... brightened by silver buttons decorated with spread eagles." Insisting that his clothes for the inauguration be fashioned solely from American-made fabric, Washington hoped to promote the young nation's industries. He understood that the United States would never achieve true independence until its factories could rival England's.

To advance the new nation's businesses, manufacturers set out to convince the public that products made in America were just as good as English ones. Advertisements that had offered "the finest dry goods just imported from London" were replaced by those boasting that American goods were by far "superior to any foreign." In an advertisement for the Boston Sail Cloth Manufactory, printed in the *Massachusetts Sentinel* on May 29, 1790, a group of local sail makers confirmed:

> We, the Subscribers, Merchants of the town of Boston, do certify That we have cloathed our vessels with the Sail Cloth made at the Boston Manufactory . . . and have made sufficient trial of it to judge of its quality and goodness. We are fully of the opinion, that it is much superior to any foreign . . . we have ever used—it wears much longer, and is not liable to mildew like imported Canvas.

Despite this enthusiasm, inexperience plagued America's manufacturers. England's factories were better designed and better equipped, and it was against English law to reveal English industrial secrets to foreign competitors. In 1790, however, a young English mechanic named Samuel Slater, trained in the manufacture of cloth, emigrated to the United States. With him Slater brought memorized plans for a new machine that could spin wispy cotton fibers into quality thread in half the time and at a much lower cost.

Once in use in the United States, this machine, along with Eli Whitney's cotton gin (1793), revolutionized the U.S. textile industry. By 1804 the young nation's cotton production had skyrocketed from two hundred thousand pounds a year to nearly seven million. The price of American-made cotton dropped to nine cents a yard (versus forty-five cents a yard for imported cloth). In 1813 New Englander Francis Cabot Lowell made textile production even faster by designing a factory that housed both thread-spinning machinery and a power loom for weaving the thread into cloth.

Other American industries—papermaking, shipbuilding, and the manufacture of hardware, carriages, farm equipment, tools, and guns—also prospered. Before long manufacturers needed new ways of selling all these mass-produced goods.

NEEDLES, PINS, BUTTONS, AND COMBS

With the same spirit of adventure that had led their ancestors to cross the Atlantic Ocean, newly independent Americans climbed mountains, forded rivers, and crossed endless plains to settle the western regions of North America. The time had come, proclaimed George Washington in 1793, to practice "the arts of peace . . . clearing rivers, building bridges, and establishing conveniences for travel." Scores of young men who hoped "to grow rich with the country" headed westward selling products. These were America's first traveling salesmen, the Yankee peddlers.

This Yankee peddler took his wagon right into his farm customer's barn to display his city-made goods—and sell them with the "art of persuasion."

With a satchel slung over his shoulder, the Yankee peddler promoted and sold the gadgets and trinkets being produced in great quantities in factories throughout New England. Isolated pioneers looked to the peddler to supply things that could not be made at home. Besides necessities such as tools, nails, and farm utensils, the peddler offered customers "kerchiefs, laces . . . earrings . . . ribbons, tapes, thimbles . . . shiny hair combs . . . buckles, buttons, and bodkins." These little luxuries, along with news from eastern towns, were welcome diversions for settlers on the frontier.

As the Yankee peddler fine-tuned the "art of persuasion," his profits grew. By the early nineteenth century, peddlers began transporting and selling larger factory-made goods—stoves, furniture, clocks, and simple farm machines. By linking East and West, the Yankee peddler helped lay the foundation for what would become America's nationwide marketplace.

BOOSTERS AND BOOMERS

Si Hawkins, breathless with excitement, read to his wife from Colonel Sellers's letter:

> Come right along to Missouri! Don't wait and worry about a good price . . . come right along or you might be too late. . . . You'll never regret it. It's the grandest country—the loveliest land—the purest atmosphere—I can't describe it; no pen can do it justice. . . . It's filling up everyday—people coming from everywhere. . . . There's enough for all. . . . You'll see! Come!—Rush!—Hurry!—Don't wait for anything!

Si and his wife, Nancy, characters in Mark Twain's novel *The Gilded Age,* typify the army of Americans who left quickly growing cities behind in search of prosperity in the West during the 1800s. These pioneers, inspired by the claims of land speculators (like Twain's letter-writing colonel), often risked everything they owned to pay for the journey.

This 1870s real estate advertisement depicted farmland in Iowa and Nebraska as picturesque and fertile. The Burlington and Missouri River Railroad, which was selling the land, offered buyers in the East free or reduced fares to get there.

America's westward expansion proved especially profitable for those who purchased large tracts of land at bargain prices, waited for property values to increase, then resold the same land to settlers at a huge profit. Vigorously advertising western towns in newspapers back East, these real estate dealers—nicknamed "boosters"—sought to "turn nowhere into somewhere." The success or failure of their advertisements often determined which towns flourished and which faded away.

Every group of speculators declared its chosen site to be "the most beautiful that Nature ever made," "the best located," "the most likely [for] the railroad to pass through," and, surely, "the best candidate for the future state capital or county seat." As one pioneer pointed out, however, enthusiastic frontier boosters "sometimes represented things that had not yet undergone the formality of taking place."

Albert D. Richardson, a journalist who toured the Midwest in 1856, explained the advertising this way:

On paper, all these towns were magnificent. . . great parks, opera houses, churches, universities, railway depots, and steamboat landing. . . . But if the newcomer had the . . . wisdom to visit the prophetic city before purchasing lots, he learned the difference between fact and fancy. The town might be composed of twenty buildings or might not contain a single human habitation. . . . Anything was marketable. Shares in interior towns of one or two shanties sold readily for a hundred dollars. . . . It was not a swindle, but a mania.

Usually a booster's first task in transforming a stretch of isolated prairie into a busy Main Street was to hire a printer to start a town newspaper. "A newspaper," wrote Richardson, is "mother's milk to an infant town."

Boosters seldom had trouble persuading a young printer to settle and set up shop. Operating a new town's press could be very profitable.

Small western newspapers often proved to be a town's best boosters.
Pictured is the staff of the **Daily Reporter** *in the Utah Territory in 1869.*

Besides publishing the local news, the frontier printer usually handled the endless stream of legal documents—contracts, deeds, mortgages—required to officially establish a town. The power of the printing press made the journalist an important member of the community.

A skillful editor never missed a chance to boost his community. In 1856, as opposing factions threatened to tear Kansas apart over the issue of slavery, Richard van Horn, editor of Kansas City's *Western Journal of Commerce,* went right on promoting his town's businesses in the paper:

> We regret that the parties have concluded to go to war and settle their differences by bloodshed; but as they have so determined, we wish to remind them that they can buy powder and lead of our merchants at St. Louis prices, and many other military supplies much cheaper.

In 1878 M. J. Cochran, editor of the *Barber County Mail,* discovered that the life of a frontier journalist could be dangerous. The citizens of Medicine Lodge, Kansas—fed up with Cochran's failure to attract new settlers—stormed the newspaper office and dragged the hapless editor into the street. The angry mob then doused him with thick molasses, rolled him in prickly prairie burrs, and ran him out of town. The message was clear—a community struggling to establish itself was no place for a bungling booster.

A town also needed good advertising if it hoped to attract the all-important railroad to its door. Boosters who succeeded in doing so found that "all was bustle and stir in the settlement; every man . . . well and full of hope."

Railroads sometimes changed their minds, however, about their proposed routes. Just as easily as the promise of the railroad coming boosted a community, a last-minute change spelled doom for it. Upon learning that the railroad would not run past their town as originally planned, the citizens of Garland City, Colorado, acted surely and swiftly. They dismantled the town's few primitive buildings, transported the pieces closer to the railroad's new route, and rebuilt. Without much fuss, they named their new town Alamosa and optimistically started boosting again.

A PENNY FOR YOUR THOUGHTS

By 1830 nearly a thousand newspapers were being published in cities and towns across the United States. Most were special-interest papers that appealed to a select group—residents in a small town, members of a political party, or people in a particular trade or profession. With a single issue costing six cents (or ten dollars for a year's subscription), few people could afford to buy newspapers. Most working people were content to browse through secondhand copies left behind in taverns, barbershops, and other public places.

In New York, publisher Benjamin Day wanted to produce a general-interest newspaper that would appeal to average Americans such as the many job seekers flooding into New York. With new paper-making machines and steam-driven presses driving printing costs down, Day could make the new newspaper affordable—one cent per copy. At that price, he predicted, he could sell as many as ten thousand copies a day. Merchants and manufacturers would jump at the chance to advertise in a paper read by so many people. And with enough paying advertisers, such a newspaper could make a profit, even at its low price.

When Day's newspaper, the *New York Sun,* hit the streets for the first time on September 3, 1833, the "penny press" was an instant hit. Besides its affordable price, the paper carried information that appealed to the common person—sensational crime coverage, detailed records of court cases, human-interest stories, and plenty of advertisements. In the first issue, editor Day stated the *Sun's* purpose:

> The object of this paper is to lay before the public, at a price within the means of everyone, ALL THE NEWS OF THE DAY, and at the same time afford an advantageous medium for advertising.

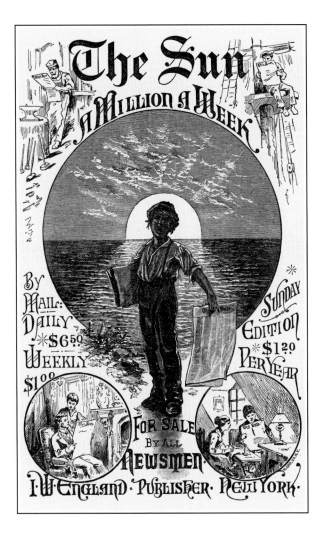

"No other newspaper published on this side of the earth has been bought and read in any year by so many men and women," boasted the New York Sun in 1883. Subsidized by advertising, the Sun was the nation's first affordable newspaper.

On city street corners, a small army of newsboys shouted "Extra! Extra! Read all about it!" Within two months, two thousand people were buying the *New York Sun* every day. Three years later, circulation had grown tenfold, making the *Sun* the most widely read newspaper in the world. Sixteen of the *Sun's* twenty-four columns of print were devoted to advertisements. The money that paying advertisers brought to the *Sun* helped keep the cost of the paper down.

The *Sun's* first penny press rival was the *New York Herald,* which debuted on May 1, 1835. The *Herald's* ambitious editor, James Gordon Bennett, was determined to attract more readers than any other paper could boast. He promoted the *Herald* as a newspaper for everyone—"the great masses of the community... the merchant, the mechanic, working people, the private family."

Bennett's style of news reporting was even more sensational than Benjamin Day's. He exposed dirty dealings on Wall Street. He printed transcripts from court trials, word for word, no matter how scandalous the testimony. In just one year, the *Herald's* circulation had reached nearly forty thousand. By 1840 Bennett boasted that his newspaper was being read by more people than all the other New York papers combined, including the *Sun.*

One of the *Herald's* most popular features was the "Personals" section, in which anyone could place a noncommercial advertisement for fifty cents. Readers found the personal ads intriguing and humorous. Pleas for wayward relatives to return home, arrangements for secret meetings, and declarations of love were plentiful. Young men and women regularly advertised for suitable marriage partners:

> WANTED,—By a young Lady, aged nineteen, of pleasing countenance, good figure, agreeable manners... and various accomplishments... a gentleman.... She will manage his household... scold his servants... accompany him to the theater... sew on his buttons, warm his slippers, and generally make his life happy. Apply... by letter, to Louisa Caroline, Linden Grove... Wedding-Ring, No. 4, Small.

Because Bennett wanted the *Herald* to carry as many ads as possible, he did not allow special headlines, elaborate type styles, or illustrations in advertisements. Instead he ran column after column of ads set in a tiny print style called agate. Although advertisers grumbled about Bennett's crammed format, they couldn't pass up the chance to have thousands of potential customers see their ads in the *Herald.*

Richard Bonner, the editor of another New York paper, devised a way to comply with Bennett's rules and still make his ads stand out from the rest. Bonner regularly advertised his own paper, the *New York Ledger,* in the *Herald.* By paying for whole columns—even full pages—of advertising space in the *Herald,* Bonner would repeat a single slogan, such as "Read the *Ledger,*" over and over until the space was filled. Sometimes Bonner arranged the tiny letters in striking formations this way:

THE NEW YORK LEDGER
THE NEW YORK LEDGER
WILL BE FOR SALE
WILL BE FOR SALE
TOMORROW MORNING
TOMORROW MORNING
THROUGHOUT THE UNITED STATES
THROUGHOUT THE UNITED STATES
AND NEW JERSEY
AND NEW JERSEY

Other times Bonner would begin a suspenseful story in one day's ad, only to stop at an exciting point in the narrative and tell readers that they would have to buy the next day's *Ledger* to find out how the story ended.

Other advertisers imitated Bonner and created their own cleverly designed ads. By arranging the miniature agate type to form larger letters and numbers, advertisers spelled out eye-catching messages in the *Herald.* This advertising technique, called iteration, became a favorite of nineteenth-century American advertisers.

Brady's Gallery, a photographic
studio, designed this eye-catching
ad in the iteration style made
popular by Richard Bonner. The
ad helped readers remember the
gallery's street address: 359
Broadway.

AN-INCH-OF-SPACE-A-MONTH

I knew that every dollar sown in advertising would return to me in tens, and perhaps hundreds, in a future harvest.
—Phineas T. Barnum, circa 1850

America's population continued to grow. Between 1815 and 1860, nearly five million new immigrants arrived from western Europe and crowded the nation's eastern cities. Machines hummed, pistols clanged, and towering smokestacks soared skyward as American manufacturers stepped up the mass production of goods.

By 1840 the age of railroad travel had begun. Nearly three thousand miles of track linked the major centers of the East. Over the next twenty years, ten times that distance—a web of thirty thousand miles of track—would crisscross the continent. Manufacturers could count on trains to deliver factory-made products to all corners of the nation more quickly and inexpensively than ever before.

The mass distribution of goods meant little, however, unless people would buy the available products. As the nation's border crept westward, manufacturers needed a way to persuade customers living at a distance from their factories to order the goods that could be shipped. Advertising was the best way to tell people about new products and services, and advertisers eagerly took up new methods.

GREATEST SHOWMAN ON EARTH

Historians credit Phineas T. Barnum with inventing the modern advertising campaign—a well-planned program of gimmicks, speeches, posters, parades, and publicity efforts used to build excitement about a new product or event. Barnum was a master showman and an expert at promoting his thrilling carnivals and other productions. "P. T. Barnum's Great Show," proclaimed one ad. "Ten Thousand Visitors!! . . . Hundreds Turned Away . . . Trained Wild Beasts! . . . 20 Trained elephants! . . . Giants, Dwarfs . . . Youthful, Daring Lady Riders!"

This kind of advance advertising stirred up such excitement that Barnum's shows were sellouts everywhere they played. No one wanted to be one of the "hundreds turned away" at the ticket window.

Barnum's approach to advertising was simple. He promoted his shows and novelty exhibits everywhere he went and as flamboyantly as possible. Not an inch of advertising space should be wasted, Barnum said. He packed his posters with fancy lettering, dramatic headlines, and lots of illustrations. His advertisements were plastered on walls, printed in newspapers, and handed out along city streets and country roads.

The name P. T. Barnum soon became synonymous with advertising. From his success, advertisers learned more effective and creative ways of promoting their products. In his 1835 autobiography,

Posters advertising Barnum and Bailey's exotic attractions, such as this one promoting a man "tattoed [sic] from head to foot," left, *drew lively crowds. The advertisement,* opposite, *warned people to get "genuine" Scott's Emulsion "as there are poor imitations."*

Barnum summed up his success as an entertainer and showman by saying: "I thoroughly understood the art of advertising."

GOOD FOR WHAT AILS YOU

The makers of patent (commercial) medicines copied many of Barnum's techniques. They spent—and earned—a fortune by advertising their tonics, pills, potions, and ointments everywhere during the nineteenth century. A medicine's name was often its first advertisement, and the best names were descriptive and memorable. Some were tongue twisters, like Radway's Ready Relief, Mrs. Winslow's Soothing Syrup, and Dr. William's Pink Pills for Pale People. Other names, like Schiffman's Asthma Cure and Carter's Little Liver Pills, told what ailment the product treated.

Like P. T. Barnum, medicine manufacturers placed their ads everywhere—in newspapers, on posters, and on signs painted on the sides of barns, mountains, and rocks along well-traveled roads.

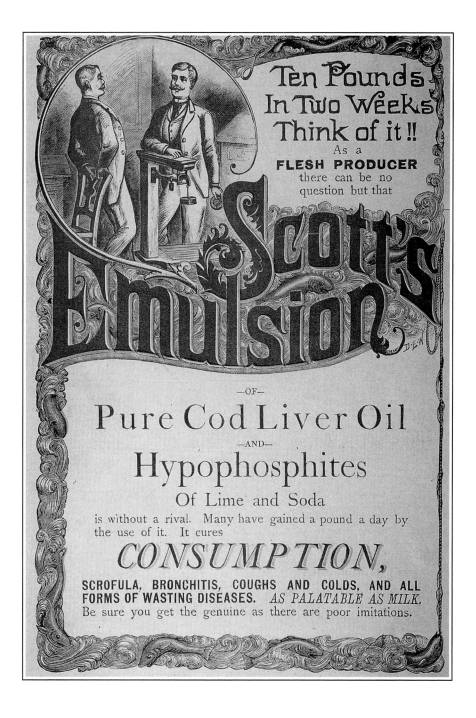

W. G. Marshall, an Englishman who toured the United States during the 1880s, described the American landscape as "daubed from one end. . . to the other with huge white paint notices . . . an endless array of advertisements puffing off the medicines of pretentious quacks." Following the Civil War, an advertiser named Charles A. Vogeler transformed a Mississippi steamboat into a floating advertisement by decorating its hull with the name of his product, St. Jacob's Oil, in twelve-foot letters that were easily visible from shore.

Another favorite technique was the news-head advertisement. By imitating a newspaper's editorial style, patent medicine makers disguised advertisements as genuine news stories. After opening with a headline like "Man Drops Dead in Street," the "article" might continue to tell how a resourceful onlooker rushed to a nearby store for a bottle of the advertised product and, with a single dose, revived the victim who had been given up for dead.

Although most people denied being fooled by this sort of outrageous tale, sales figures indicate that during the late 1800s, people spent more money on patent medicines than on any other product. In 1850 Americans spent $3.5 million on patent medicines. Five years later, that amount had risen to a whopping $75 million.

Allcock's Porous Plasters supposedly protected people from being too warm or chilly and "cured" them of colds, rheumatism, nervous disorders, and other troubles. "Let no solicitation," warned this ad in the 1890s, "induce you to accept a substitute."

Most advertisements were less blatant about the ingredients of a product than this ad for hair tonic. When this ad ran in 1886, most people did not realize that cocaine is a dangerous, addictive drug.

THE
BEST HAIR DRESSING
COCOAINE
It kills Dandruff, promotes the Growth of the Hair, cures Scald Head and all Irritation of the Scalp.

Patent medicines promised something for everyone. City people looked to them to remedy the ill effects of office and factory work, which offered little fresh air and exercise. And for people in rural areas with no doctor nearby, buying a bottle of patent medicine was a welcome break from brewing one's own home remedies. What few people realized, however, was that many patent medicines contained large amounts of alcohol or dangerous narcotics—and little real medicine. In their pursuit of a cure-all, many Americans became addicted to the products.

Sales of patent medicines grew steadily until the early twentieth century, when studies confirmed the dangers of taking them. In 1906 Congress passed the Pure Food and Drug Act, which required the makers of patent medicines to accurately list all active ingredients on product labels.

OPPORTUNITY KNOCKS

In 1843 Volney C. Palmer, a blustery Philadelphian with a knack for selling things, pictured an important—and profitable—place for a man of his talents in America's expanding marketplace. Declaring himself "duly accredited . . . to receive advertisements" on behalf of "the best newspapers published in the United States and Canada," Palmer set up shop as a middleman who could link merchants who wanted to advertise with newspapers that had space to sell. Palmer is considered America's first advertising agent.

Although cities were growing rapidly, until 1920 the majority of Americans still lived in farming regions. Palmer figured that big-city manufacturers could sell more goods if they could reach people in these rural areas. He wrote letters to every newspaper editor he could locate and offered—for a fee—to find merchants willing to purchase advertising space in the paper. Then Palmer approached merchants, explaining how advertising would lead to great profits.

Although Palmer called himself an advertiser's agent, he actually worked for—and was paid by—the newspapers. He made no effort to place an ad in newspapers most suited to it. He made no guarantee that the advertiser would pay the newspaper, nor that the ad would attract any new customers for the merchant. Once Palmer had a merchant's promise to buy advertising space, he collected his fee from the newspaper and considered his job done.

Palmer's fondness for wheeling and dealing earned him—and advertising—an unsavory reputation. No one was sure just how Palmer's system worked, or even if advertising was the key to selling more goods. Despite these doubts, few advertisers wanted to lose out on the big profits Palmer promised, so they continued doing business with him. By 1850 another half dozen such agencies had sprung up in New York and Philadelphia. Because these agents used the same shady methods as Palmer, the public's general mistrust of advertising hung on.

ADVERTISING'S FIRST CHAMPION

In 1869 a new breed of agent—one determined to establish advertising as an honorable profession—arrived on the scene. New Hampshire native George P. Rowell, like Volney Palmer, realized that finding advertising space for merchants could be very profitable. Rowell also recognized, however, that no merchant would continue to advertise unless the ads helped to sell more goods. It was a waste of the

The nation's first bona fide advertising agency, George P. Rowell & Co., sold clients "an-inch-of-space-a-month" in each of one hundred newspapers.

advertiser's money, for example, to promote farm equipment in city newspapers, since city people had no use for it. Rowell also knew that newspapers could not stay in business unless merchants paid their advertising fees on time. His agency guaranteed that newspapers got paid.

George Rowell developed new advertising methods. First, he researched newspapers from all over the country and found out how many people read each one. Papers with the most readers could charge higher fees for advertising space—because more people would see the ads. Then, with his own money, Rowell purchased large sections of blank space in several different kinds of newspapers. Because Rowell paid ahead of time, he earned hefty discounts from the newspapers, which liked receiving their fees "up front."

Rowell then resold the space in smaller portions to advertisers. For one hundred dollars, a business could purchase "an-inch-of-space-a-month in one hundred newspapers." (An inch was approximately twelve lines of type.) During Rowell's first year in business, he invested six hundred dollars in newspaper space—and made two thousand dollars reselling it.

Sometimes an advertiser would ask Rowell's opinion about the best way to advertise. "Honesty is the very strongest point," he advised. "Come down with the facts, boldly, firmly, unflinchingly. Say directly what [the product] is, what it has done, what it will do. . . . Say flatly 'the best' or say nothing." As a fair and reliable agent, Rowell developed satisfied customers who continued to do business with him year after year.

In 1888 Rowell founded *Printer's Ink,* a trade magazine for the developing advertising industry. The publication offered a place for agents to exchange ideas, learn more about advertising techniques, and develop greater professionalism.

ADVERTISING GROWS UP

By 1875 advertising agents were no longer simply middlemen who arranged to buy and sell space in newspapers. They had gradually assumed the job of creating ads for the manufacturers who hired them. As print technology improved, agencies started to experiment with different type styles, designs, and headlines.

Before long many agencies discovered that some employees were better at one part of ad making than another. Some employees were good writers; others could draw. Business executives were good at hammering out the details of a contract.

Around 1880 John E. Powers became the first advertising specialist. As a copywriter, Powers created only the words for ads, nothing else. In a crisp, clean, and simple style, he wrote short sentences that formed little essays about advertised products. Powers stated his uncomplicated approach this way:

> The first thing one must do to succeed in advertising is to have the attention of the reader. That means to be interesting. The next thing is to stick to the truth, and that means rectifying whatever's wrong in the merchant's business. If the truth isn't tellable, fix it so it is. That is about all there is to it.

What Powers called his "talking style of writing" proved very popular with a public that had grown weary of advertisements that made outlandish claims.

Next, agencies began studying the best ways to promote a client's product. Which advertisements were reaching the most people? What sort of people read which newspapers? What kinds of ads did people like to read? Which elements were more effective: words or pictures? And, most importantly, which advertisements would make people go out and buy the product? These questions gave rise to the advertising agency's research department.

Between 1880 and 1900, American manufacturers more than doubled the amount of money they spent on advertising—from forty million dollars to almost ninety-six million. Many of advertising's most influential agencies were launched during this period, including Philadelphia's N. W. Ayer and Son, New York's J. Walter Thompson agency, and the Chicago firm of Lord and Thomas. A virtual alphabet soup of organizations for advertising professionals followed, including the AACA (Associated Advertising Clubs of America, 1904) and the AAAA (American Association of Advertising Agencies, 1917). Many women entered the growing industry, some of them forming the AWNY (Advertising Women of New York) in 1912.

ASK FOR IT BY NAME!

Advertising!
    —multimillionaire publisher
Cyrus H. K. Curtis, when
asked the secret of his success
in 1878

W e were dirty and smelly," writes historian Jack Larsen of our colonial ancestors. "Early nineteenth-century Americans lived in a world of dirt . . . and pungent smells. . . . Men's and women's working clothes alike were often stiff with dirt and dried sweat." In summer, people bathed in the nearest stream or river after a day's work. A quick dip and a brisk rub with a cloth removed most of the grime. In winter, it was often too cold "to get wett all over." But since everyone smelled pretty awful, unpleasant body odor was barely noticed.

As American cities became more crowded, personal cleanliness took on new importance. In close quarters like apartment houses and factories, body odors became offensive, and poor sanitation bred disease. Gradually people began to associate poor hygiene with low social status and low moral character. "He that neglects his person and dress," wrote William Alcott in 1935, "will be found lower in the scales of morals . . . than he who pays a regard to cleanliness."

Mass production and new inventions also changed attitudes toward hygiene. Through the early nineteenth century, soap making—a time-consuming and messy job—was done at home. Americans were more than happy to turn the task over to factories, which could produce soap in large quantities at low cost. And with new conveniences like indoor plumbing, bathtubs, and water heaters, people quickly discovered that they *liked* feeling clean and comfortable.

Soon Americans were washing regularly, using soap and water. To ensure that people kept buying soap, manufacturers had to promote cleanliness, not as a luxury but as a necessity. By the turn of the century, advertisements for toothpaste, toothbrushes, mouthwash, shampoo, and soap were everywhere. But how could a manufacturer ensure that people chose its product over the competition?

WHAT'S IN A NAME?

For most of the nineteenth century, the small-town general store was the commercial heart of the United States. Grocers stocked goods in bulk—pickles in barrels, hefty slabs of soap, sides of cured bacon, and sacks of sugar and flour. Selection was limited and there was little, if any, effort to control the quality of the products being sold. Shoppers shooed away gnats to scoop broken crackers from a barrel or to fill a sack with milled flour.

Although some goods carried the manufacturer's name, there was usually no distinction between one product and another. The manufacturer that could give its product a distinctive brand name would have an advantage. With persistent and widespread advertising, a company could tell why its brand of soap (or bacon, or flour, or pickles) was the best, and why the consumer should choose it.

Before the advent of brand-name packaging, general stores stocked goods in bulk.

In 1852 the Union Paper Bag Machine Company patented a device that made paper sacks. Gradually bags imprinted with brand names and logos replaced the containers that people normally supplied for themselves when shopping. Soon logos began to appear on boxes, jars, and tins. In 1887 a Minnesota grocer named Patrick Towle began offering his blend of maple syrup and cane sugar in small tin containers shaped like houses. The result was the still-popular Log Cabin syrup.

Around 1900 the National Biscuit Company (Nabisco) began selling its crackers in boxes that featured an "In-Er-Seal" lining. From then on, cardboard cartons with waxed paper lining became the standard package for goods like cookies and crackers. The success of the company's Uneeda Biscuits (as in "you-need-a biscuit") spawned similarly named products, including Uwanta Beer, Itsagood Soup, and Ureada Magazine. None of these brands survived very long, however.

Although brand-name packaging did not completely end bulk selling, it changed the American marketplace. Shoppers, influenced by clever advertising and attractive packaging, began to demand certain brands instead of others. If grocers and wholesalers wanted to stay in business, they had to carry the brands that people wanted.

U.S. law permitted manufacturers to register a product's name and logo, making it illegal for anyone else to copy them. In 1871 only 121 manufacturers had registered brand-name trademarks with the U.S. Patent Office. By 1905, 10,000 such trademarks had been registered.

Many of the brands introduced in the late nineteenth century remained popular a century and more later. These enduring brands include Ivory Soap (1879), Levi Strauss jeans (1853), Campbell's Soup (1869), Hires Root Beer (1876), Quaker Oats (1877), Coca-Cola (1886), Kodak cameras (1888), Post Grape Nuts (1898), and Kellogg's Corn Flakes (1907).

An early Coca-Cola ad promotes the drink's ability to "ease the Tired Brain— soothe the Rattled Nerves and restore Wasted Energy to both Mind and Body." This company's slogan changed over the years, but its logo remains the same.

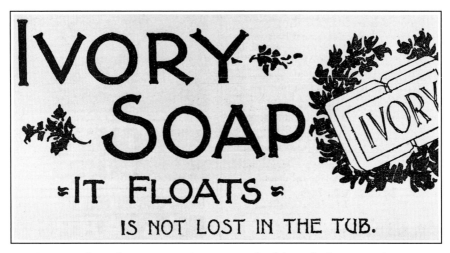

By the time this ad ran in 1894, everyone had heard of Ivory, "the soap that floats."

"IT FLOATS"

In 1875, when letters began arriving from customers demanding more of "the soap that floats," executives at Proctor & Gamble were baffled. The soap company offered several kinds of soap. Did one of them float?

After some investigation, they discovered that a few weeks earlier a factory worker had left a batch of the company's "white soap" churning for longer than usual. The result was soap with extra air whipped into it, causing it to bob up to the surface of the water when dropped in the washbasin.

Renamed "Ivory" and promoted with the slogan "It Floats," the new product took the market by storm. By 1890 thirty million cakes of Ivory Soap were being sold every year.

Because soap could be manufactured easily and inexpensively, many companies made it. This meant stiff competition for Proctor & Gamble. If the Cincinnati soap maker wanted people to buy Ivory Soap instead of other brands, it would have to convince the buying public that Ivory was the best soap on the market. So Proctor &

Gamble created a distinctive identity for Ivory—using a process called differentiation.

Differentiation suggests that the advertised brand of a product is somehow superior to all other products of its kind. "Accept No Substitutes!" and "Beware of Imitators" advertisements warned consumers. An Ivory Soap advertisement in *Literary Digest* on May 26, 1906, alerted shoppers:

> Is there more than one kind of Ivory Soap? No, but there are a hundred imitations. A dishonest grocer will give you one of these and say, "This is Ivory," or "This is just as good." Do not accept it unless it is stamped IVORY. The shape of the cake and the appearance of the wrapper may be similar, but the name cannot be used on any but the genuine.

Ads like this not only urged consumers to ask for a brand by name but also encouraged them to tell the manufacturer if their local grocer did not sell the brand. In return manufacturers often awarded free samples to loyal customers who snitched on the local grocer.

Another important marketing technique was segmentation, by which manufacturers created special versions of a product for different users and different purposes. For example, one soap promised to give women "a skin you love to touch." Another was the only soap that could make "little babies coo with delight." Still another boasted "a germ-destroying agent" able to handle man-sized grit and grime.

Segmentation boosted sales by convincing shoppers that one kind of soap was simply not enough to keep the whole family properly washed. By the turn of the century, scores of new laundry detergents, shampoos, spot removers, and other bubbling, scrubbing household cleaners were brought to life by segmentation.

REACHING A WIDER AUDIENCE

Newspapers were still the most popular way to advertise. But because newspapers were published for local readers, they did not provide the kind of nationwide exposure advertisers wanted. To promote their products nationally, manufacturers began to distribute small advertisements, about the size of a postcard, called trade cards.

New printing technology and the compact size of trade cards made it possible to print them in color and distribute them widely at a reasonable cost. Some manufacturers tucked trade cards in packages leaving the factory. Others mailed them to local grocers, who then handed them out to shoppers.

Most cards featured a colorful scene—of a factory, bridge, or tall building—on one side and a sales message on the other. On the sales side, advertisers sometimes linked patriotic symbols with their products, often with humorous results. A trade card put out by the Eagle Pencil Company of New York, for instance, featured the Statue of Liberty atop her pedestal, holding not her torch but a handful of

This trade card depicts a well-dressed gentleman easily pushing the New Easy Lawn Mower under the approving gaze of the Statue of Liberty.

Eagle pencils. On other companies' trade cards, Lady Liberty could be found standing on a giant spool of silk thread or on a box of wafers. Uncle Sam—in his familiar red-and-white striped trousers and blue waistcoat—appeared on trade cards for everything from Boston Baked Beans to farm machinery.

Collecting trade cards became a popular pastime, much like modern stamp or baseball card collecting. People saved cards in albums, exchanged them with friends, and displayed them as decorations in their homes. The trade card fad lasted into the early twentieth century. Then advertisers discovered a new, more powerful advertising medium—the mass-circulation magazine.

THE RISE OF POPULAR MAGAZINES

Once trade cards had demonstrated the effectiveness of national advertising, local newspapers lost much of their appeal for advertisers. National magazines like *Scribner's, Harper's,* and the *Atlantic Monthly* provided a much wider readership. They included articles and stories that spoke to people no matter where they lived.

At first the publishers of these magazines refused to carry advertising. They considered it unsuitable for their readers, whom they called the "prosperous and intelligent classes of society." Without the financial support of advertising, however, magazines had to depend on high-price subscriptions to stay afloat. When publishers finally did begin accepting advertisements, they printed them only in rear sections of the magazines, where they wouldn't interrupt the flow of stories and articles.

In 1882 a Philadelphian named Cyrus H. K. Curtis was busy publishing a small weekly magazine for farm families. Three of the four pages of his *Tribune and Farmer* provided helpful information for farmers. The remaining page was a "Lady's Page," with items of interest to farm women.

Curtis did all the writing and editing for the magazine himself. When his wife, Louisa, declared that she could write a much better page for women than he, Curtis invited her to give the job a try. When she showed exceptional talent as a writer, Curtis decided to sell the small farming magazine and keep only the page for women. In 1883 the husband and wife team launched *Ladies' Home Journal,* a national magazine whose motto was (and still is) "Never Underestimate the Power of a Woman."

While other magazines of the day charged three or four dollars for a yearly subscription, *Ladies' Home Journal,* by carrying advertisements, could charge just twenty-five cents a year and still make a profit. Advising readers on family life, cooking, fashion, and child care, each issue also came jam-packed with ads for new products that could help women in their household tasks. Unlike its competitors— who targeted a smaller, more elite audience—*Ladies' Home Journal* was written for ordinary Americans.

Curtis believed that the magazine could reach thousands—maybe millions—of women in every part of the country. His sharp business sense, along with Louisa Curtis's expert editorial skills, proved him correct. Circulation climbed quickly from 100,000 readers to nearly 500,000 in just six years.

Advertisements in *Ladies' Home Journal* featured the multitude of brand-name products born around the same time as the magazine. Early in his career, Curtis posed a question at a gathering of national advertisers:

> Do you know why we publish the *Ladies' Home Journal?* The editor thinks it is for the benefit of American women. This is an illusion. . . . I will tell you; the real reason, the publisher's reason, is to give you people who manufacture things that American women want and buy a chance to tell them about your product.

By 1900 advertising experts estimated that women made approximately eight out of every ten purchases for the home. By advertising in *Ladies' Home Journal,* advertisers were speaking directly to the country's most influential consumers—women.

Louisa Curtis and her husband, Cyrus, published the **Ladies' Home Journal,** *the first-ever magazine exclusively for women. The magazine helped advertisers target a specialized audience—women.*

In 1889 Louisa Curtis had retired and turned the popular magazine over to a new editor, Edward Bok. Bok, a self-educated Dutch immigrant, proved to have a remarkable understanding of "the intelligent American woman." It was under his direction that *Ladies' Home Journal* became the first American periodical to claim one million readers per issue. When the magazine introduced an attractive two-color cover, sales skyrocketed, and money from advertisers poured in. "The fact must never be forgotten," wrote Bok in one editorial, "that no magazine published in the United States could give what it is giving to the reader each month if it were not for the revenue which the advertiser brings to the magazine."

Bok viewed *Ladies' Home Journal* as an instrument for promoting health and enlightenment for American families. With money paid by advertisers, he could afford to publish the work of some of the world's finest authors, including Louisa May Alcott, Rudyard Kipling, Sir Arthur Conan Doyle, and Mark Twain. In fact Bok is credited with introducing fine literature to middle-class America.

The success of *Ladies' Home Journal* inspired other popular publications to drop prices and turn to mass advertising. In turn-of-the-century parlors across the United States, *McClure's, Munsey's, Collier's,* the *Saturday Evening Post,* and other mass-circulation magazines could be found alongside *Ladies' Home Journal.*

THE LARGEST STORE
IN THE WORLD

*Don't be afraid you will make a
mistake. We receive hundreds of
orders every day.... Tell us
what you want in your own way,
written in any language, no
matter whether good or poor
writing, and the goods will
promptly be sent to you.*
—ordering instructions,
Sears, Roebuck and Co., 1897

Richard Warren Sears wondered what to do about the unclaimed carton of gold watches that sat in the depot. As railroad agent for Redwood Falls, Minnesota, Sears had accepted the delivery on behalf of the local jeweler who, it turned out, had not ordered the watches and refused to pay for them.

Using part of his modest salary, Sears paid for the wayward watches and decided to sell them himself. A week later, with every watch sold and a tidy profit in his pocket, Sears realized two things: he was a good salesman, and a good salesman could make a lot of money.

In 1887 Sears moved to Chicago, Illinois, and started the R. W. Sears Watch Company. There he met Alvah C. Roebuck, a watch-maker. Though they had almost opposite personalities, Sears and Roebuck realized they made a good team. Sears, an outgoing sales-man, and Roebuck, a quiet craftsman, formed a partnership.

Sears and Roebuck quickly learned the lesson of volume buying. By placing big orders with manufacturers, they paid a lower price per item and could pass those savings on to customers. Not only did volume buying work for watches, but also for ready-made clothes, shoes, corsets, furniture, and musical instruments. Anything that could be mass-produced could be bought in large quantities and resold for a profit.

In 1886 the U.S. population totaled about fifty-eight million. Sixty-five percent (nearly thirty-eight million) lived in rural areas. However, farm life had changed considerably by the late nineteenth century. Labor-saving devices like the reaper and threshing machine had increased the farmer's output and lessened the farmer's workload. The harvest no longer fed just the farmer's family but also yielded crops to sell in the growing national marketplace. All this meant new prosperity for the farmer and more time to enjoy it. Writer Hamlin Garland recalled looking over his family's Iowa farm at harvesttime:

> We stood before it at evening when the setting sun flooded it with crimson . . . our hearts expanded with the beauty and mystery of it—and back of all this was the knowledge that its abundance meant a new carriage, an addition to the house, or a new suit of clothes.

Rural life was still one of isolation, however, and the farmer's only source of supplies was the local shopkeeper, who often charged high prices. Richard Sears realized that America's farm families represented an untapped market for all the products pouring from the nation's factories.

As a railroad agent, Sears had often handled shipments from Chicago's large mail-order house, Montgomery Ward. He knew that mail-order selling generated big profits by offering residents low prices, a wide selection of goods, and the convenience of shopping at home. He also thought that mail-order shopping would be popular with isolated rural customers.

By 1895 Sears had designed a 532-page mail-order catalog that featured everything from fishing rods to saddles to baby carriages to stoves. He wrote nearly every one of the catalog's ads himself, saving the expense of paying an advertising agency. Lower costs meant bigger profits for Sears and Roebuck.

Sears created his advertisements with the rural family in mind. His breezy, familiar style made people feel as if he were speaking to them directly. "We extend a hearty welcome to every patron to visit us should you ever come to Chicago," wrote Sears. "You can readily find us, and you will find it well worth your while to go through our big building." Throughout the Midwest, "Mr. Sears and Mr. Roebuck" were soon dubbed "the farmers' friends." Rural customers welcomed the opportunity to buy new and exciting products by mail from a "friend."

By eliminating all middlemen, Sears erased the miles between the big city and the farm. "You can sit down by your own fireside," he wrote in 1897, "and with our catalog you have all the advantages of a metropolitan store." Even isolated country folks, who tended to be suspicious of big-city businesses, trusted Sears.

By purchasing—and later manufacturing—goods in large quantities, Sears was able to offer very low prices on the products farmers needed and wanted. "If you don't see what you want, write and tell us," Sears wrote in the catalog. "We will find anything you need." His words were magical to farm families who were accustomed to making do. Low prices, selection, and a money-back guarantee proved to be a surefire selling program for Sears and Roebuck.

As Sears's share of customers grew, local retailers watched their own businesses slack off. In retaliation some small-town merchants offered rewards to children for turning in the family's Sears catalog, which the shopkeepers then added to their woodpiles. Local store owners spread rumors that belittled the quality of mail-order goods and warned customers about sending money to far-off places. None of these efforts succeeded. After just one year, Sears, Roebuck and Company had turned a tidy profit of sixty thousand dollars.

Richard Sears was not the first American to do business by mail, but he was the most successful. His catalog—called a "masterpiece of advertising"—separated Sears from his competitors.

GETS YOU THERE AND GETS YOU BACK

Of all the new consumer products available at the start of the twentieth century, the automobile was king. The new invention did, however, meet with some resistance. For stable owners, harness makers, and streetcar workers, the coming of the automobile meant lost business and fewer jobs.

People accustomed to horse-drawn buggies and wagons enjoyed seeing a motorist stuck in the mud or stalled. "Get a horse!" critics advised as their neighbors in goggles and touring coats desperately tried to start their cars. In 1902 Theodore Roosevelt—an acclaimed adventurer and the first American president to ride in a car—took the precaution of having the automobile he was riding in followed by a horse and buggy in case of an emergency. Behind each doubt, however, was a natural curiosity about the horseless contraption: how it worked, and what it had to offer the common person.

The first automobile advertisements were newspaper accounts of races run by car hobbyists. As more articles appeared, skeptical spectators gathered to see what all the fuss was about. Gradually bigger and bigger crowds came to the races, excitement grew, and people started thinking about someday driving an automobile of their own.

Car makers added to this free publicity by running paid advertisements in newspapers and magazines. The earliest ones stressed the automobile's safety, durability, and ease of operation. "So simple a boy of 15 can run it," promised a 1903 car ad in the *Saturday Evening Post*. The ads also pointed out that an automobile could go where railroads could not, required less care than a horse, and could travel

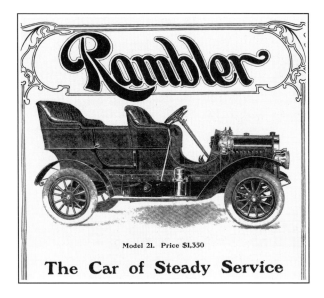

Model 21. Price $1,350

Early car manufacturers—such as Thomas B. Jeffrey & Company, maker of the Rambler—stressed that cars were just as reliable as horses.

long distances without needing a rest. Rural folks, the advertisements suggested, could escape the monotony of farm life in a car, and city dwellers could enjoy "hours of pleasure in God's great open spaces." Automobiles were for everyone.

By 1899 some eighty independent automakers were vying for the consumer's business. Most of these manufacturers were bicycle enthusiasts who built cars one at a time in their garages and backyards. Cars made in this time-consuming fashion were far too expensive for the average person, however.

Henry Ford, a self-taught machinist from Dearborn, Michigan, came up with a plan to make automobiles affordable for everyone. Hoping to earn enough money to start his own manufacturing company, Ford competed in races and used the free publicity to promote his plan to investors. (Throughout his life, Ford maintained that it was foolish to pay for advertising when you could get it free through publicity.)

By 1908 Ford had produced a no-frills automobile that he named the Model T. At a price of $850 (most other cars sold for around $1,500; a custom-built Oldsmobile cost $2,750), the Model T sold quickly. Ford wasn't satisfied. He insisted the price could be lowered even more by improving mass production.

Ford broke automobile making into a step-by-step process and assigned each factory worker one job to do over and over. He set up a series of motorized conveyers to carry each unfinished car past each worker, who installed the windshield or door or wheels—whatever his designated job was.

By 1915 Ford's system could fully assemble a Model T in just ninety-three minutes, and his factory was turning out one thousand cars a day. The price of a Model T plunged from $850 to $440. As Ford continued to fine-tune his assembly-line system, the price plunged again—to $265 by 1924. By then nearly half of all the cars in the world were Model T Fords. There seemed to be no way for Ford's competitors to challenge his dominance of the automobile industry.

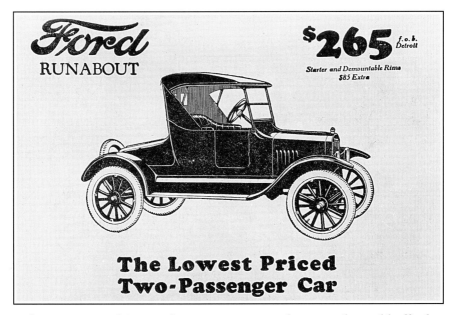

When Henry Ford invented a way to mass-produce cars, he could afford to drop his prices and began to outsell every one of his competitors. Advertisements—such as this one from 1924—helped him get the word out.

In 1908 five independent automakers—Chevrolet, Buick, Oldsmobile, Pontiac, and Cadillac—had merged to form General Motors (GM). Other mergers, bankruptcies, and buyouts further reduced the number of American automobile makers. In 1923 GM came under the direction of Alfred P. Sloan, whose goal was to beat Ford in sales.

Henry Ford, meanwhile, still shunned paid advertising. The few ads he did approve stressed his Model T's reliability, sturdiness, ease of operation, and low price—but never the car's style. Here, thought Sloan, was the key to capturing some of Ford's share of the automobile market. As GM's president, he established the car industry's first art and color division, a department that concentrated exclusively on automobile style and design.

GM offered cars in a choice of colors with the latest "duco lacquer finish." A 1928 Chevrolet advertisement boasted of cars that were "brilliant in their modish new colors—alluring in their distinguished

The "Bigger and Better" Chevrolet of 1928 boasted "impressive performance," "delightful comfort," and "distinctive style" rather than the low price of a Ford.

smartness." Ford's other rivals—Lincoln, Packard, and Duesenberg—followed GM's lead, advertising cars with "unusual attractiveness," "a spark of color, . . . a flash of modish lines," and "custom-built exclusiveness without excessive cost."

Next Sloan introduced a concept called planned obsolescence to American manufacturing. With this strategy, manufacturers made small changes in a car's design from one year to the next, making the previous year's model seem outdated, unfashionable, and "obsolete." Almost all the changes involved only the look of the car, not its engine or its performance.

By emphasizing these so-called improvements in their advertisements, automakers persuaded car buyers that they needed to own more than just any old automobile. They needed to have the latest model. By taking advantage of trade-in deals and "E-Z payment plans" offered by car manufacturers, average Americans were able to drive the biggest, newest, most stylish automobiles available—whether they could afford them or not. Ford's rivals saw sales figures rise steadily as Ford's fell.

Henry Ford considered "the necessity to restyle the most popular car in the world [his own Model T, of course] . . . a lot of hogwash," but the success of his competitors forced him to rethink his policy. In 1927 the brand-new Ford Model A debuted, heralded by ads claiming it was "Everything you want or need in a Modern Automobile . . . beauty of line and color—flashing pick-up and ease of control that put new joy in motoring."

RADIO DAYS

On November 2, 1920, a crackle of airwaves ushered in the age of radio, as station KDKA in Pittsburgh, Pennsylvania, broadcast election returns in the presidential race between Warren G. Harding and Ohio governor James M. Cox. Teachers, civic leaders, and social reformers viewed radio as a powerful instrument that could educate, inform, and enlighten the public.

The invention of the radio enabled listeners to tune in to stations all across the country. Advertisers had an effective new medium.

The idea that radio might also carry advertisements disturbed some Americans. In 1922 Secretary of Commerce Herbert Hoover denounced commercial radio, saying that it was "inconceivable that we should allow so great a . . . service to be drowned in advertising clatter." Radio airwaves were considered public property, and regulations prohibited "any attempt to make radio an advertising medium" for profit.

Advertisers, however, realized that radio was perfectly suited for reaching consumers with sales messages. As an advertising medium, radio offered something completely new. With the flip of a switch, the advertiser could deliver a sales pitch to thousands of consumers at the same time, all in the comfort of their own homes. As more powerful transmitters were built and networks of stations spanned the country, the opportunity for nationwide advertising was obvious and exciting.

Attempts to keep radio ad free did not last long. Radio networks, like newspapers and magazines, could not operate without financial support. Since companies were willing to pay to advertise over the airwaves, regulations about radio advertising were changed. Direct selling over the radio was still prohibited, but advertisers and broadcasters devised a system that would achieve the same results. In the new system, companies like Kodak, General Foods, and Proctor & Gamble would sponsor—pay all the costs of producing—radio programs. In return sponsors could mention their products at the beginning and end of broadcasts.

General Mills, makers of Wheaties (the "Breakfast of Champions"), sponsored one of the most popular radio serials of the 1930s, *Jack Armstrong, the All-American Boy*. Every day, kids rushed home from school, tossed books aside, and switched on the radio to follow their hero's latest adventures. As the announcer introduced the day's episode, he never missed an opportunity to remind the audience of the show's sponsor:

> Wheaties, Breakfast of Champions, brings you the thrilling adventures of Jack Armstrong, the All-American Boy. . . . A very special welcome for the fellows and girls who are hearing this program for the very first time today. We hope you'll all get a lot of thrills and pleasure out of Jack Armstrong's newest adventure and that you'll make the acquaintance of those extra-good Wheaties flakes right away. You know, right now, at the beginning of a new school year and at the start of a brand-new Jack Armstrong series, is a mighty fine time to start making Wheaties your year-round breakfast dish. . . . And now, Jack Armstrong, the All-American Boy.

The repeated linking of a product's name with the name of the radio show firmly connected the two in the listener's mind. Advertisers made the most of the association, using contests and promotional giveaways. Charles Crowley recalls how, as a boy, he munched his way through "bowl after bowl of Wheaties" to collect enough box tops to earn his own "Jack Armstrong Egyptian Whistle Ring" and secret code book. "All the kids were crazy for them. If Wheaties were good enough for Jack Armstrong, they were good enough for us," he remembers.

Promotional giveaways were not only used to plug cereal to kids. Homemakers who faithfully followed daily "soap operas"—ongoing melodramas nicknamed for the soap companies that sponsored them —collected coupons from soap wrappers, cracker packages, and jar labels. In exchange the coupon clippers received samples of hand cream, cleansers, and cookbooks galore.

Special offers and contests kept product names in front of audiences long after the radio was switched off. Catchy jingles that had appeared as rhymes and slogans in print advertisements were set to music and played on the radio. "It's amazing," said one advertising agent, "how the silliest things stick in one's mind."

Radio shows and advertising even helped "Americanize" immigrants new to the United States. Many people learned to speak English by listening to the radio and imitating common American expressions and slogans. With no reading required, radio was the ideal medium for advertising to everyone, regardless of economic and social background.

ON BORROWED TIME—THE ROARING TWENTIES

The United States emerged from World War I as an industrial giant with plenty of products to sell. Business was booming, the mood was high, and Americans, having had enough of the world's problems, embarked on a decade-long buying spree.

Americans had always viewed buying on credit (making a small down payment for an item, then paying the rest in monthly installments, plus interest) as a "far-reaching evil," something to avoid. Before 1900 few things besides houses and land were purchased with credit.

However, at the turn of the century, as mass production brought expensive items (like automobiles) within reach of the average person, the stigma once associated with buying on credit began to fade.

Early twentieth-century advertisements for sewing machines, "electric suction cleaners" (vacuums), book collections, refrigerators, and stoves explained to modern consumers how they could "buy now, pay later." The exact words might change from one ad to another ("only a reasonable first payment is required," "low prices, liberal terms," "pay the easy way"), but the advertisements all meant the same thing—consumers no longer had to wait to have the things they wanted. "Just ask," one advertiser told shoppers, "and the dealer will explain our easy purchase plan."

As the stock market climbed to previously unimagined heights, people even started to buy stocks on credit, then used profits that only existed on paper to make more investments. The frenzy of accumulating more of everything—more products, faster cars, more excitement and fun—helped usher in the Roaring Twenties.

ALL THAT JAZZ

The goal of advertising in the 1920s was to promote a modern lifestyle, along with the message that everybody should have the latest high-tech products. The most modern images of the era were created in a style called art deco. Borrowing aspects from a variety of historical art forms—especially Egyptian and Aztec architecture—art deco featured sleek lines, slender human figures, and simplified geometric shapes with rounded edges. The Empire State and Chrysler Buildings in New York (both completed in 1930) are classic examples of the art-deco style.

Using bright colors and art-deco styling, artists of the 1920s created advertisements that not only attracted but also held the reader's attention. Words were kept to a minimum. Often the product's name appeared alone with a beautiful illustration. Advertising that used inviting yet subtle images to persuade buyers was called "soft sell."

In this art-deco style ad of 1927, a stylish woman wears sleek Goodrich zippers on her shoes.

Art-deco style advertisements radiated elegance, wealth, and sophistication. The glint of chrome trim seen on automobiles and fast trains was a prominent feature of such advertisements. In a limited-run issue of the *Saturday Evening Post* in 1930, an ad for Alcoa aluminum included aluminum printing ink that made the metallic details in the ad gleam. Prosperity was all the rage until 1929 . . . and then the bottom fell out.

HARD SELL FOR HARD TIMES

When the stock market crashed in October 1929, the U.S. economy tumbled rapidly into a downward spiral. Businesses failed and banks closed. By 1933 the unemployment rate in the United States had reached 25 percent (almost fourteen million people). Many people lucky enough to keep their jobs took drastic cuts in pay. The Great Depression was on.

Hard times plagued advertising, as they did most industries. Many agencies lost their best accounts, while those clients who remained trimmed their advertising budgets to the bone. Advertisers who had spent nearly $3.4 billion in 1929 devoted less than half that amount to advertising in 1933. Consumer spending slowed to a crawl as lenders began repossessing many ill-advised purchases made on credit.

In an effort to stimulate business, advertisers turned from the soft sell to the "hard sell"—high-pressure sales techniques designed to convince people to continue to buy even after they were broke. As humorist Will Rogers described advertising in 1933, "It makes you spend money you don't have for something you don't want."

The new ads provoked anxiety and guilt among consumers, arguing that the failure to buy certain products marked them as bad

The stock market crash of 1929 took a toll on American pocketbooks and morale. Spending decreased sharply in its wake.

parents or low-class slobs. Ads for toilet paper, for example, suggested that poor performance in school or on the job was a result of "harsh toilet tissue." Poor-quality photographs, usually the horror-stricken faces of those caught in embarrassing situations, replaced the elegant art-deco illustrations of the 1920s. Advertising historian Ralph Hower describes the decline of advertising during the depression years:

> The shrieking headlines, gross exaggeration, and even downright deceit which appeared had no parallel except the patent medicine advertising of the nineteenth century, while the use of pseudo-scientific arguments and appeals to emotion and appetite. . . violated previously accepted standards of decency.

Manufacturers tried everything to improve sales. In the late 1920s, an organization called the Cleanliness Institute began showing up in newspaper articles. The institute's goal, it explained, was to encourage

Few Americans could afford luxuries during the Great Depression of the 1930s, so advertisements started hawking everyday items such as soap as necessary to proper health.

people to exchange poor hygiene habits for healthy ones. Beginning in 1930, "experts" from the Cleanliness Institute stepped up their campaign to instruct the public about the benefits of a daily bath—with soap—and of washing one's hands several times a day. The institute supplied textbooks for schools at a reduced price, sent health-care professionals to speak in classrooms, and published teachers' guides to improve hygiene education.

Its official-sounding name and its public-spirited activities made the Cleanliness Institute seem important and scientific. In reality, however, the organizers of this group were members of the Association of American Soap and Glycerin Producers—manufacturers who wanted people to buy more soap.

The activities of the Cleanliness Institute reinforced what consumers were also reading about in advertisements: foot fungus, halitosis (bad breath), gingivitis (gum disease), "undie odor," dandruff, and other afflictions that could turn a person into a social outcast faster than you could say "Beeee Ohhhh!" (body odor). All these ailments, advertisers promised, could be prevented or fixed by using their products. Many advertisements included a "doctor's recommendation."

While these aggressive tactics clouded advertising's reputation once again, they still got people to go out and buy products. By 1938, as the depression was nearing its end, polls showed that consumers considered soap a necessity of life—second only to food. Advertising had once again proved itself to be a powerful weapon in influencing human behavior.

IN WAR AND PEACE

Advertising is the foot on the accelerator, the hand on the throttle, the spur on the flank that keeps our economy surging forward.
    —NBC president Robert Sarnoff, 1958

When the United States entered World War II in December 1941, everyone pitched in. The nation's factories stopped making radios, appliances, and automobiles and instead began producing the planes, weapons, and tanks needed by the military. In 1942 members of the advertising community formed the War Advertising Council, placing all of their talents and creative resources at the government's disposal.

With the same persuasive techniques advertisers used to sell commercial products, the War Advertising Council rallied Americans on the home front to conserve, reuse, or do without those materials needed by the nation's soldiers. Posters encouraged people to carpool and conserve precious fuel, reminding motorists, "When you ride ALONE, you ride with Hitler!" Another poster promoted the efforts of American women who worked in the defense industry: "My husband's in the army.... I'm in the shipyard.... We're in this war together." Graphic images of terrified mothers protecting their babies from outstretched

Nazi arms drove home the consequences of an enemy victory.

Such public service messages filled up newspapers, magazines, and radio airwaves. At the same time, advertising professionals who served on the War Advertising Council managed to squeeze in a good word for their peacetime clients. Vegetable canners urged people to free up crops for the armed forces by growing their own tomatoes, corn, radishes, lettuce, and cabbage in "Victory Gardens." Bell Telephone asked customers not to tie up long-distance lines so that servicemen and servicewomen could call loved ones. One New England insurance company encouraged people to "Give a pint of life insurance" to promote blood donations desperately needed on the front lines.

These ads not only inspired patriotism at home but also helped gain the goodwill of the public. Advertisers hoped that when the war was over, shoppers would remember the contribution that advertising and industry had made to the war effort.

THE AMERICAN DREAM

Having sacrificed during the Great Depression and World War II, Americans of the postwar period were ready to settle down and enjoy peacetime prosperity. Bank books burst with nearly $140 million in savings, which consumers were ready to spend. The nation's advertisers were just as eager to advise them how to spend it.

Through advertisements, people learned of the latest trends in food, fashion, household appliances, automobiles—even houses. William Levitt's real estate development, "Levittown" on New York's Long Island, offered veterans and their families affordable housing. After running just one advertisement in the *New York Times,* Levitt sold fourteen hundred homes, each with a backyard for the kids to play in.

And there were plenty of kids. Some seventy-five million "baby boomers" were born between 1946 and 1964. Families needed food, diapers, clothes, shoes, books, soap, furniture, tires, fuel for their automobiles, and appliances of every size, shape, and purpose to run an efficient, modern household.

This full-page ad for "Levittown," which ran in the New York Times *on August 2, 1953, sold fourteen hundred homes.*

Advertising during the 1950s delivered the promise of stability and prosperity that Americans craved. It also bolstered the idea of the United States as one giant coast-to-coast shopping center—using a new medium for spreading advertisers' messages. Television fever swept the nation.

DON'T TOUCH THAT DIAL

Long before World War II, scientists from several countries had investigated the possibility of transmitting not only sound but also pictures through the air. By the 1940s, people were crowding in front of department store windows and in neighborhood taverns to watch the first demonstration television sets. By 1950 Americans had purchased nearly four million televisions of their own and continued to buy them at the astonishing rate of one hundred thousand sets each week.

As TV's popularity grew, sponsors abandoned radio and headed in droves for the television studio. By the late 1940s, nearly every major

Viewers crowd a storefront in 1953 to catch a glimpse of television and its fascinating ads.

advertising agency had added a department just to handle TV advertisements. In 1949 advertisers spent about $12 million promoting their products on television. By 1951 they were spending more than ten times that—almost $128 million—to televise their messages to Americans.

Television's combination of sight and sound made it perfectly suited for advertising. Like radio, television could deliver the advertiser's message to millions of homes at one time. Television also allowed viewers to see advertisers conduct live demonstrations of their products on the air. For example, the makers of a disposable razor demonstrated its effectiveness by shaving the whiskers off a lion. The Timex company dropped watches from cliffs, strapped them to high-powered boat propellers, and zapped them with electric shocks. No matter how rough the test, announcer John Cameron Swayze always retrieved the watch and showed the audience that a Timex watch "takes a licking and keeps on ticking." To prove how sturdy its products were, Tonka Toys had an elephant stand on top of one of its toy trucks. The truck passed the weight test, and sales of Tonka Toys soared.

Television also offered advertisers a great opportunity to have celebrities endorse products on the air. Entertainers who projected honesty and sincerity were the most sought after. Popular singer Dinah Shore encouraged viewers to "See the U.S.A. . . . in your Chevrolet" just before throwing a big kiss to the audience at the end of her show every week. Film star Ronald Reagan, who would one day become president of the United States, plugged lightbulbs and appliances for General Electric.

Television advertising started out much as radio had, with programs bankrolled by sponsors. On behalf of their corporate clients, advertising agencies hired creative talent—writers, directors, actors, and technicians—to produce television shows that met with clients' approval. Agency copywriters also wrote commercials to be shown during the sponsors' programs.

This era of sponsor-controlled programming offered viewers some of the finest drama and comedy ever broadcast—it has been called the "Golden Age" of television. TV's *Playhouse 90, Kraft Television Theater, Motorola Playhouse,* and the *U.S. Steel Hour* showcased the work of fine scriptwriters such as Tennessee Williams, Paddy Chayevsky, and Rod Serling.

Corporate sponsorship proved troublesome, however, because some advertisers wanted total control over the content of the shows they paid for. No sponsor wanted a story to suggest anything negative about what was being advertised. Writers had to be careful not to interfere with the sponsor's goal—to sell more products. Television historian Erik Barnouw explains:

> Most advertisers were selling magic. . . . In the commercials there was always a solution as clear-cut as the snap of a finger: the problem could be solved by a new pill, deodorant, toothpaste, shampoo, shaving lotion, hair tonic, car, girdle, coffee, muffin recipe or floor wax.

Sometimes sponsors demanded that writers and directors tailor shows exactly to their advertising needs. One early detective show, *Man against Crime,* was sponsored by the makers of Camel cigarettes. The tobacco company's executives absolutely prohibited the writers to suggest anything negative about smoking. Only "good guys" could smoke; crooks never did. Characters couldn't cough because coughing might remind viewers of the possible connection between cigarette smoking and lung disease.

In another instance, the same cigarette maker insisted that writer Rod Serling change one of his scripts. The sponsor wanted Serling to find substitutes for the words *lucky* and *American,* because the American Tobacco Company, makers of Lucky Strike cigarettes, was one of its biggest competitors. Creative people like Serling resented this kind of censorship.

Still, sole sponsorship of early television shows did earn customer loyalty. Research showed that people bought the products advertised

The crooks who tied up actor Ralph Bellamy in this scene from Man against Crime *didn't smoke Camel cigarettes. Only good guys did.*

during the most popular shows. Realizing television's power as an advertising medium, the networks that owned television studios eventually decided to produce shows themselves and collect advertising fees from several advertisers rather than let one sponsor control an entire time slot.

This new system was called spot advertising, and it worked very much like newspaper and magazine advertising. If a company wanted to advertise on television, it paid the network to run a commercial. By selling "time" to multiple advertisers in slots of a minute or so, networks could air several different commercials throughout a program. Because the costs were lower for a small spot of advertising time (compared to sponsoring an entire show), more companies could afford to advertise on television.

A rating system (developed by the Nielsen company) tracked people's television-watching habits and rated programs according to the number of viewers who watched them. The higher a show's Nielsen rating, the more it cost advertisers to air commercials during that program. Regardless of cost, most advertisers were willing to pay the price for television's effective, far-reaching influence.

KEEP AMERICA BEAUTIFUL

Shortly after daybreak on a sweltering Sunday in 1958, a small group of angry citizens of New Mexico, saws in hand, followed the highway out of town to the first of seven billboards they had targeted for destruction. The vigilantes swiftly flattened the huge advertisements one after another until all that remained was a pile of rubble.

Their actions, though illegal, were met by popular approval from the community at large. Some neighbors protested that the group had not cut down enough billboards. Others felt cheated. It seems they had been planning a billboard bonfire of their own, but someone had beaten them to it. No arrests were made in the case, and the ax-wielding activists were never identified by name.

This backlash against advertising was by no means new, but the protests had never been more pronounced. People were beginning to question the effects of advertising not only on American society but also on the environment. One important result was the Highway Beautification Act of 1965, which prohibited the placement of billboards within 660 feet of federally supported roads.

In 1952 *Printer's Ink* reported the results of polls conducted to determine just what consumers thought about the advertising industry. One poll showed that 41 percent of Americans considered advertising to be misleading. Another poll revealed that 80 percent of Americans believed that advertising made people buy things they didn't need or couldn't afford.

To add to advertising's woes, around this same time several novels about the advertising industry hit bookstores. A few were written by "insiders"—people who worked in advertising—and generally depicted the business as a "cheap, phony, vicious racket" that disregarded the truth and disrespected the public's intelligence. In movies like *The Hucksters, Will Success Spoil Rock Hunter?* and *Lover Come Back,* Hollywood depicted advertising agents as materialistic, overly ambitious "go-getters" who would stop at nothing to claw their way to the top.

Another book, *The Hidden Persuaders* by Vance Packard (1958), accused advertisers of using secret tactics to "brainwash" consumers. Packard claimed that subliminal advertising (hidden messages buried in ads) made consumers spend money without knowing why they were doing it. Packard's theories, though never proven, made people more suspicious of advertising than ever before.

Despite negative opinions, advertising had become a major American industry that employed thousands of people. By the late 1950s, three dynamic leaders with fresh ideas emerged from the ranks. Leo Burnett, David Ogilvy, and William Bernbach, each using his own brand of originality, helped bring advertising into a new era. The creative revolution started by these three set a standard for advertising that still stands.

SORRY, CHARLIE!

Leo Burnett was nothing like the advertising agents portrayed in novels and Hollywood films. As historian Stephen Fox describes him:

> Burnett was not much to look at. . . . He was short and pear-shaped, with sloping shoulders and a comfortable paunch . . . a freshly rumpled suit . . . [that] attracted cigarette ashes and other debris. . . . His face looked lopsided. . . . Nobody would take him for an advertising man.

But the shy, mumbling Burnett and the agency he headed created some of the most memorable advertising campaigns of the 1950s and 1960s.

Burnett got a late start in the advertising business. During the 1930s, as the editor of a newsletter for the Cadillac division of General Motors, Burnett worked with some of GM's top copywriters and discovered his own talent for creating advertisements.

In 1935, when Burnett was forty-four years old, he sold his house, cashed in his life insurance policy, and opened his own advertising firm, the Leo Burnett Company, in Chicago. It was a risky thing to do at the height of the depression, when few companies could afford to pay an agency to develop ad campaigns. Burnett described the advertising of the 1930s as "dull, stupid, uninteresting." He had no use for coupon-clipping promotions, giveaways, or contests. Likewise, he felt that "scientific research" on Americans' buying habits was vastly overrated.

Burnett believed that the way to impress the American public was to give a product a distinct "personality." In creating ads, said Burnett, the advertiser had to discover what was special about a product and then, using truth, interesting artwork, and lots of humor, tell the customers, "This is what we have. This is what it will do for you. This is how you get it." By 1959 the small midwestern agency that Leo Burnett started with $50,000 was handling nearly $100 million in clients' advertising money.

The Burnett agency is best known for the cartoonlike characters it created, many of which are still familiar to consumers. For the Minnesota Valley Canning Company, Burnett's creative team came up with the Jolly "HO-HO-HO" Green Giant—an ad campaign that was so effective that the canned food processor changed its name to the Green Giant Vegetable Company. The Jolly Green Giant quickly became part of American popular culture.

Among the other characters created by Burnett's agency were Poppin' Fresh (the Pillsbury Doughboy), Tony the Tiger for Kellogg's

Created by Leo Burnett's advertising agency, Poppin' Fresh (the Pillsbury Doughboy) tee-heed his way into American living rooms—and kitchens.

Product personalities appealed to American consumers. A car-tuna Charlie had tuna lovers stocking their cupboards with Starkist brand tuna.

Corn Flakes ("They're grrreat!"), and the Rice Krispies sprites Snap! Crackle! and Pop! Burnett's creation, the finicky cat, Morris, refused to eat anything except Nine Lives cat food, and Charlie, an overeager fish, tried numerous ways to be selected by Starkist Tuna, only to be told time after time, "Sorry, Charlie!"

People instantly accepted the Burnett "critters." They appealed to the American fondness for folksy, colorful humor and didn't make people feel as if they were being tricked into buying products. According to Burnett, "Anyone who thinks that people can be fooled or pushed around has an inaccurate and pretty low estimate of people— and he won't do very well in advertising."

A TOUCH OF CLASS

Born in London in 1911 and educated at some of England's finest schools, David Ogilvy was as different from Leo Burnett in appearance as one man could be from another. Tall, charming, well spoken, and impeccably groomed, Ogilvy tried several occupations before settling into advertising. Until 1938 he worked as a chef in Paris, a door-to-door salesman in England, and a trainee in a London advertising agency, then emigrated to the United States and got a job conducting opinion polls for the Gallup company.

In 1948 Ogilvy combined his varied experiences and opened the advertising firm of Ogilvy, Benson and Mathers. The agency started with a few small accounts and with only modest success. In 1951, however, the Hathaway Company of Vermont hired Ogilvy's agency to create advertisements for their shirts. Ogilvy set out to create a sophisticated image for the small shirt company and chose a distinguished-looking male model to appear in the Hathaway ads.

Ogilvy's creative instincts told him to surround the "Hathaway Man" with a mysterious air. On the way to the first photo session, Ogilvy stopped at a local drugstore and purchased a black eye patch for the model. Ads pictured the man with the eye patch involved in a variety of activities—playing music, painting, conducting an orchestra,

"*Never wear a white shirt before sundown!*" *says Hathaway. After sundown? Wear this. About $11.*

"Every man should own at least one <u>opulent</u> white shirt"
—*says Hathaway*

and examining priceless works of art. Overnight "the man in the Hathaway shirt" became one of the most recognized men in America. Readers of the *New Yorker* magazine checked its pages each week to see what new hobby the Hathaway Man was up to. Once the Hathaway Man became popular, the Vermont clothier couldn't keep up with the demand for its shirts.

Ogilvy's ads could not be placed in any one advertising category. On one hand, he followed the soft sell theory—creating an image of distinction, sophistication, and mystery for the product. But Ogilvy, a trained researcher, also knew that people wanted to know about a product's advantages. So his ads also followed the "claim" or "reason why" method of advertising: listing convincing reasons why consumers should buy the advertised brand. Ogilvy explained:

> I always pretend that I'm sitting beside a woman at a dinner party, and she asks me for advice about which product she should buy. . . . I write down what I would say to her. I give her facts, facts, facts. I try to make them interesting, fascinating, if possible, and personal. I don't write to the crowd. I try to write from one human being to another. . . . The best ads come from personal experience.

The successful Hathaway Man campaign attracted a lot of business for Ogilvy's advertising agency. In 1958 Maxwell House Coffee ("Good to the Last Drop") signed on as a client. Eventually the agency also created commercials for Mattel's Barbie Doll, Shell Oil, American Express, Dove Soap ("1/4 moisturizing cream"), and Pepperidge Farm cookies and breads.

In 1963 Ogilvy wrote a best-selling book called *Confessions of an Advertising Man*. After retiring he wrote a second book called *Ogilvy on Advertising*. The firm he began in 1948 has grown into a worldwide powerhouse with eighty-three offices in forty-three countries. It employs 1,500 people and remains one of the most successful agencies in the history of advertising.

BREAKING ALL THE RULES

The Volkswagen Beetle looked nothing like the long, flashy, tail-finned American automobiles of the late 1950s. Short and round, the German-made car resembled a bug on wheels. Its "air-cooled" engine was located in the rear, where other cars had trunks, and its trunk was located under the front hood.

The manufacturer of the Beetle knew that selling the strange-looking vehicle to Americans, who liked their cars luxurious and spacious, would not be easy. Volkswagen would need just the right agency to handle its American advertising plan.

The New York firm of Doyle Dane Bernbach (DDB) was the kind of advertising agency Volkswagen needed. The company's president, William Bernbach, had earned a reputation as one of the most creative

Volkswagen's "Think small" slogan startled Americans used to hearing about "bigger and better." The humor was refreshing—and sales skyrocketed.

minds in advertising. His offbeat sense of humor, love of art, and re-spect for the intelligence of American consumers helped him create ads that were unique, attractive, and effective. "The most important thing," Bernbach believed, "is to be fresh and original."

Bernbach thought that ad agencies relied too much on scientific research. "They know all the rules. . . . But . . . they forget that adver-tising is persuasion, and persuasion is not a science, but an art. Advertising is the art of persuasion."

Like Leo Burnett, Bernbach never underestimated the intelligence of the American consumer. He believed that people didn't need to be tricked into buying things. As long as a product was as good as the ad said it was, Americans would use it and keep on buying it. "Don't be slick," he advised the artists and copywriters at DDB. "Tell the truth."

Bernbach believed in honest advertising and said that he would never advertise a product he didn't believe in. "Nothing makes a bad product fail faster," he said, "than a great advertising campaign."

The campaign that DDB came up with for Volkswagen's Beetle re-mains one of the most famous series of ads ever created. The ads were simple. Even in magazines printed in color, the ads for the Beetle used a single black-and-white photograph. The unusual use of black and white helped "perform the first function of an ad," which was, Bernbach claimed, "to stop the reader." Each ad contained a pic-ture, along with a single bold headline and a brief explanation of one or two things that made the car special.

One full-page ad featured the tiny automobile with a two-word headline: "Think small." The message below the picture explained why the odd little car was becoming popular:

> Our little car isn't as much of a novelty anymore. . . . The guy at the gas station doesn't ask where the gas goes. No-body even stares at our shape. In fact, some people don't even think getting 32 miles to the gallon is going great guns. Or using five pints of oil instead of five quarts. Or never needing anti-freeze. Or racking up 40,000 miles on a

set of tires. That's because once you get used to some of our economies, you don't even think about them anymore. Except when you squeeze into a small parking space. Or renew your small insurance. Or pay a small repair bill. Or trade in your old VW for a new one. Think it over.

Bernbach's refreshing style helped change the way people thought about small automobiles and about advertising. U.S. sales of the Beetle shot up from 19,000 cars in 1950 to nearly 1.6 million in 1968, and DDB established itself as a top-notch agency.

AND THE WINNER IS . . .

On September 26, 1960, John F. Kennedy, then a United States senator, and Vice President Richard M. Nixon faced off in the first of four televised debates leading up to that year's presidential election. More than seventy million Americans tuned in and saw a handsome, suntanned Kennedy who appeared relaxed and confident. Nixon, on the other hand, looked pale, tired, and ill at ease under the studio lights.

Following the debates, a survey was taken of two groups of people: those who had watched the debates on television and those who had listened on radio. Having seen the candidates, the television viewers thought Kennedy was the better debater. The radio audience, who had only *heard* them, thought Nixon had done the better job.

In November Kennedy narrowly defeated Nixon for the presidency. Many people attributed Kennedy's victory to the attractive image he projected on television. Some people began to believe that political candidates, like products and ideas, could be "packaged, advertised, and sold" to the public.

The Kennedy-Nixon debates also reconfirmed something advertisers already knew. Television's ability to bring dynamic visuals of political candidates (and breakfast cereals, toys, appliances, and the latest fashions) right into the consumer's living room made it the ideal advertising medium.

During the 1960 presidential campaign, families gathered around the television to watch the debates between John F. Kennedy and Vice President Richard M. Nixon.

THE TIMES THEY ARE A CHANGIN'

Kennedy's election was the first in a series of fundamental changes in American society—and advertising. As people turned away from the conformity of the 1950s and embraced greater individuality in the 1960s and 1970s, advertisers realized they needed to appeal to a more diverse audience. Slowly but surely, advertising's attitudes about African Americans, Hispanic Americans, physically challenged citizens, and others broadened. Advertisers not only began paying more attention to these groups as consumers but also began casting a wider variety of people as models and actors in ads.

A product's image could be easily updated to attract a newly defined audience. The manufacturer of Levi Strauss blue jeans, for example, gave its nineteenth-century clothing a whole new personality. The company had advertised its blue jeans as heavy-duty work clothes for farmers. The updated approach presented Levi Strauss denim pants and jackets as fashions. Urban men and women enthusiastically adopted the look, and the company's sales figures exploded.

For many years, women in advertisements were portrayed in domestic situations. In the 1960s, that started to change. A 1990s Nike "Just Do It" ad shows a very different sort of woman.

Another way in which advertising changed during the 1960s and 1970s was in its depiction of women. Advertisers had long realized that women were the most likely consumers to buy their products. Even so, advertisements often reinforced the attitude that women were not as smart or as capable as men. A woman's greatest assets were her beauty and her suitability as a wife and mother, ads often seemed to say. Until a woman chose this soap or that cereal, she was less than perfect.

But many women in the 1960s were rejecting the notion that they were inferior to men. As women claimed more control over their lives and sought greater opportunities in business, science, technology, and other fields, ad makers began depicting women working in these areas, in jobs traditionally associated with men.

One of the first arenas of widening opportunity for women was in sports. Beginning in the 1970s, women athletes such as tennis player Chris Evert scored great financial successes by endorsing products. Then, in the 1980s, Nike began putting more women in its ads for athletic shoes. The ads showed women playing hard and fast, sweating, and thriving on competition just as much as men did.

NEW AND IMPROVED

He who has a product to sell
And goes and whispers in a well,
Is not so apt to get the dollars,
As one who climbs a tree and
hollers.

               —Anonymous

Many basketball fans well remember superstar Michael Jordan suspended in midair, high above the rim, ready to drive home a slam dunk. Even before Jordan retired in 1999, he spent a good deal of time working as one of advertising's greatest success stories. As spokesperson for several product lines (including a line of underwear, hot dogs, breakfast cereal, and athletic shoes), Jordan earns some forty million dollars a year—more than ten times the salary he had earned as a player for the Chicago Bulls.

Why are manufacturers willing to pay Jordan so much? The answer is simple. People buy the products Jordan endorses. His fame and prestige are invaluable assets in advertising, where the name of the game is selling.

Why did Anheuser-Busch agree to pay the Fox television network two million dollars to air a thirty-second beer commercial during the 1999 Super Bowl (that's more than sixty thousand dollars per second!)? Because advertising during the Super Bowl, the most-watched TV show of the year, can make sales of Anheuser-Busch products skyrocket.

Advertising speaks to us from newspapers and magazines, by radio and television, and on giant billboards that dot—and sometimes clutter—our landscape. Studies have found that each day the average American sees or hears almost two thousand advertisements. According to one conservative estimate, a typical American child is exposed to nearly one million advertisements before entering first grade.

Some social scientists say that advertising, by creating artificial desires, exerts an often unhealthy influence over the choices Americans make. Following advertising's lead, a nation of productive, self-sufficient people has become discontented, forever in search of something bigger, better, faster, and easier.

Advertising's defenders, on the other hand, point out that ads introduce people to new and better products and create educated consumers. The result, they insist, is the high standard of living Americans enjoy.

Advertising's effect on our culture—our values, beliefs, habits, and customs—sometimes seems very powerful. Does advertising reflect American society as it is? Or does it portray life as we wish it could be? Does its power extend beyond reflecting society? Does it shape society? Can a television commercial that makes us laugh—or a print ad that delights us with words and pictures attractively arranged on a page—compel us to buy things we really don't want or need? Do ads influence us to accept ideas we might otherwise reject? Responsible citizens and consumers who raise questions like these find no ready answers.

THE ROAD AHEAD

What lies ahead for advertisers and the consumers they want to influence? Most people agree that the future of advertising lies with the Internet. The Internet was launched in 1969 as a communications

In an Internet ad, the publisher of this book does some advertising of its own. Interested customers can view books of all subjects online.

network supporting U.S. military research being done at four American universities. More than thirty years later, the Internet is used every day by an estimated 200 million people worldwide.

Some say the Internet has become the most effective advertising medium ever. Consumers can find plenty of free information online about almost anything, including a vast array of products and services. It's easy, fast, and convenient to shop while cruising the World Wide Web. Just look at the ads, "click" if you're interested, and pay by credit card without leaving your home.

Online advertisers use the Internet in many ways. One is to sponsor an online activity such as a chat group for people with a common interest. These advertisers focus on that common interest in specialized advertisements. Banners or buttons link users to sites where they can buy related products or find related information.

Other online advertisers sponsor free, multiplayer games. These games attract thousands of prospective customers every day. People who want to play must register personal information such as e-mail address, age, interests, and hobbies. This information gives the advertiser the reward of an instant, defined customer base.

Perhaps the most important feature of Internet advertising is that it allows an advertiser to interact with an Internet user instantly. For example, a car manufacturer might structure an Internet site to allow a potential customer to "build" his or her own sports car by selecting features from a list of options. Once the car has been created, the customer can immediately forward the information to a local dealer who, in turn, contacts the customer with a price. The advertiser hopes the quoted price will draw the customer into the showroom.

Clearly the Internet's suitability as an advertising medium far surpasses anything advertising agents of the past could have imagined. But only time will reveal the extent of the possibilities. One thing is certain, however, says historian David Cohn. Whether in the past, the present, or the future, advertising reveals a great deal about who we are. Through advertising, Cohn says:

> One finds out how men lived . . . . Here are the clothes they wore; the books they read; the medicines they used; . . . the songs they sang; the plows they walked behind; the furniture that stood in their homes; . . . the clocks that tick men's lives away, and the tombstones that mark the end.

Just as we look back at early advertisements to glimpse Europeans journeying to the New World, people many years in the future can look back at us through our ads. Ads are artifacts—objects we have made and left behind us—that reflect our identity and values. In them we hear the hum of the clocks that tick our days away and the rhythm of the songs we sing—the measure of our times.

*In this illustrated ad for Pears'
Soap from 1887, a monkey shaves
a dog while a cat watches.*

SELECTED BIBLIOGRAPHY

Andrist, Ralph K. *American Century: One Hundred Years of Changing Life Styles in America.* New York: American Heritage Press, 1972.

Andronik, Catherine M. *Prince of Humbug: A Life of P. T. Barnum.* New York: Atheneum, 1994.

Assael, Henry, and C. Samuel Craig, eds. *Printer's Ink: Fifty Years (1888–1938).* New York: Garland Publishing, 1996.

Barnouw, Erik. *Tube of Plenty: The Evolution of American Television.* New York: Oxford University Press, 1975.

Bowers, Q. David, ed. *Early American Car Advertisements.* New York: Bonanza Books, 1966.

Cohn, David L. *The Good Old Days: A History of American Morals and Manners as Seen through the Sears, Roebuck Catalog, 1905–the Present.* New York: Simon and Schuster, 1940.

Emery, Michael, and Edwin Emery. *The Press and America.* 7th ed. Englewood Cliffs, NJ: Prentice Hall, 1992.

Fox, Stephen. *The Mirror Makers: A History of American Advertising and Its Creators.* New York: William Morrow, 1984.

Franklin, Benjamin. *The Autobiography and Other Writings by Benjamin Franklin.* Edited by Peter Shaw. New York: Bantam Books, 1982.

Galanoy, Terry. *Down the Tube: Or Making Television Commercials Is Such a Dog-Eat-Dog Business It's No Wonder They're Called Spots.* Chicago: Henry Regnery Press, 1970.

Ad styles may change over the years, but people's desire to look their best never does.

Goodrum, Charles, and Helen Dalrymple. *Advertising in America, The First Two Hundred Years.* New York: Harry N. Abrams, 1990.

Halberstam, David. *The Fifties.* New York: Villard Books, 1993.

Hornung, Clarence P., and Fridolf Johnson. *200 Years of American Graphic Art: A Retrospective Survey of the Printing Arts and Advertising since the Colonial Period.* New York: George Braziller, 1976.

Hoy, Suellen. *Chasing Dirt: The American Pursuit of Cleanliness.* New York: Oxford University Press, 1995.

Jones, John Philip. *What's in a Name? Advertising and the Concept of Brands.* Lexington, MA: Lexington Books (D.C. Heath & Co.), 1986.

Marchand, Roland. *Advertising the American Dream: Making Way for Modernity.* Berkeley, CA: University of California Press, 1985.

Margolin, Victor, Ira Brichta, and Vivian Brichta. *The Promise and the Product: Two Hundred Years of American Advertising Posters.* New York: Macmillan, 1979.

"Mr. Sears' Catalogue." *The American Experience.* Written and produced by Edward Gray, Mark Obenhaus. 59 min. Alexandria, VA: PBS Videotape, 1989.

Norris, James D. *Advertising and the Transformation of American Society, 1865–1920.* New York: Greenwood Press, 1990.

Ogilvy, David. *Ogilvy on Advertising.* New York: Vintage Books, 1985.

Pope, Daniel. *The Making of Modern Advertising.* New York: Basic Books, 1983.

Presbrey, Frank. *The History and Development of Advertising.* Garden City, NY: Doubleday, Doran and Company, 1929.

Schudson, Michael. *Advertising, The Uneasy Persuasion.* New York: Basic Books, 1984.

Shorris, Earl. *A Nation of Salesmen.* New York: W. W. Norton, 1994.

Strasser, Susan. *Satisfaction Guaranteed.* New York: Pantheon Books, 1989.

Tedlow, Richard. *New and Improved: The Story of Mass Marketing in America.* New York: Basic Books, 1990.

Vinikas, Vincent. *Soft Soap, Hard Sell: American Hygiene in an Age of Advertisement.* Ames, IA: Iowa State University Press, 1992.

Watkins, Julian Lewis. *The 100 Greatest Advertisements: Who Wrote Them and What They Did.* New York: Dover Publications, 1959.

INDEX

ACKNOWLEDGMENTS

Photographs and illustrations used with permission of Corbis-Bettmann, pp. 2–3, 6, 20, 23, 30, 33, 35, 43, 44, 49, 56, 63, 64; North Wind Picture Archive, pp. 8, 11, 14, 15, 22, 26, 32, 34, 40, 54; Print and Picture Collection, The Free Library of Philadelphia, p. 12; Museum of Fine Arts, Boston. Reproduced with permission. All rights reserved, p. 16; National Archives, pp. 17, 66, 83; The Metropolitan Museum of Art, p. 18; IPS, pp. 29, 37, 88, 91; Brown Brothers, pp. 42, 55, 58, 62; Archive Photos, pp. 46, 72; Reuters/Sue Ogrocki/Archive Photos, p. 50; Levittown Public Library, p. 68; Daily Mirror/Corbis-Bettmann, p. 69; American Advertising Museum, pp. 75, 76 (both), 78, 80, 84; Sporting News/Archive Photos, p. 86; Corbis, p. 90.

Front cover: Corbis-Bettmann
Back cover: Northwind Picture Archive; Archive Photos
Cover design by Edward C. Mack